On Music Education, Psychology & Different Abilities

Sofija Zlatanova

On Music Education, Psychology & Different Abilities

Copyright © 2023 by Sofija Zlatanova

ISBN: 978-1-7338618-7-8

All rights reserved. No part of this publication may be reproduced in whole or in part, stored in a retrieval system or in an information storage, or transmitted in any form or by any means, electronic, mechanical, photography, scanning, recording or otherwise, without the written permission of the publisher.

I dedicate this book to my younger brother, Boshko Zlatanov, who was accepted by some prestigious schools abroad for Music studies, and who wanted to study Music and Song Production.

However, he decided not to accept the offers, because of the opportunities I had been given to pursue my Music studies. He thought that financially it would not be possible for our parents to send both of us to study abroad.

I later found out about this. I thank him, I admire him, and I respect him.

Table of Contents

Introduction 1

Chapter 1 5
Global Composers: choosing the right school
and method for the violin student

Chapter 2 33
On Composers, Analyzing & Application

Chapter 3 59
Keeping a healthy, creative brain by employing
musical composition as a method of treatment

Chapter 4 87
Music and Different Abilities

Chapter 5 127
What Does it Mean to be Critical?

Chapter 6 147
Crafting For and Working with the Gifted Multimedia Student

Chapter 7 169
Behavior-teaching Strategies, Developed Using Music, Art,
and Composition

Assignments and Exercises 187

Chapter 8 207

Gallery of images 209
Acknowledgments 321
Bibliography 323

We cannot all do great things. Yet, we can all try to do small things with lots of love"

Mother Teresa

The Great Humanitarian and Saint

To Sofia from Valentina—a Preface with love

...A random meeting, a conversation, a radio interview, then another interview: and in a moment one thinks of this gentle girl sitting in front of me. The Universe, through her name, determined her life-path, or rather, the mission in her life's journey.

Sofia Zlatanova—*Wisdom and Value.*

The accomplished concert musician, humanitarian, my one-time fellow citizen, here she comes with new challenges, with a new project, in the baggage she has carried with her since her childhood, the viola as an inseparable companion and protector. Sofia has wisely decided to share all her emotional, valuable wealth with all those who need the healing music molecule. She created a small peace, with lots of love, step by step, to insight and development in the process of self-awareness, as well as mind and body healing.

On Music Education, Psychology and Different Abilities is an inspiring, proven educational tool that gives the answers how to reach every human being through music in order to dive fearlessly into the mutual process of giving and receiving—through pure love.

Valentina Samac

Journalist and host of Radio Skopje—National Radio-Television, North Macedonia

Introduction

Welcome to my class, my lecture, my philosophy—the music, the teaching, and the healing.

My *Multicultural Inclusive Methodology Perspective* promotes healing, and educational growth teaches everyone with different abilities equally and inclusively, based on the student's strengths, personal goals, and creativity.

I want the student to learn with the teacher's help, not by mimicking. My students take their time, and the deadline for the work to be submitted can be adjusted, based on the student's emotional well-being. Educators should consider cultural differences in the way that students learn and express themselves.

My methodology applies to both teachers and students. It is to let the students learn by themselves, with educational material presented and created by the teacher, allowing the students to play and learn, with some assistance and application from the teacher. That is the healthiest and fastest way for the students to learn and grow.

I don't want the student to succeed just by copying, and doing what the teacher wants, but to let the student collaborate in designing the lesson plans and timings.'

I do not want to use recommendations to approve someone's work: I believe in the student, the process, and the outcome.

I do not support general exams, because each student's brain is different. Its uniqueness lets him or her stand out in one of the two hemispheres of the brain, left or right—the Art one, and the analytical and mathematical one.

The well-being of the whole person is essential to me. The holistic approach is what I aim for, and at the same time, learning. The expressive arts using music can serve as 'medicine', by using selected pieces by composers, matching these with each individual's creative health style.

I particularly want to portray classical music's influence on our personal lives, and how its notes overflow like a watercolor, depicted through our imagination and thoughts. We become the composition, and, like an artist's painting, we are exhibited and presented to others who may not understand us, understand our personality, or accept our character.

Moreover, a 'miracle' might happen: a teacher who will carry us and understand the way that the marvelous story of the great composers has drawn us—the great composers who, like the most enchanting poem, have poured the notes, their every moment, into the most magnificent compositions: such as Beethoven's Ninth Symphony, which will forever remain in the history of music as one of the most powerful, mysterious, and profound works that have not only painted our lives, but have affixed their seal to the universe, leaving music infinite and unrivaled among all the universe's phenomena.

"Music represents power; she can wake up all our senses as the cure for our soul. Thanks to her, all sounds become meaning. A sound is not just a sound anymore, but a word, a music sentence that is born in the greatest works and interpretations by the greatest artists and composers."

Sofija Zlatanova

Global Composers: choosing the right school and method for the violin student

Music educators and violin teachers must have a background in knowing, respecting, and implementing the different musical styles, or creating our own. There are some selected schools we can choose, or use to recreate our technique, based on the student's hands and structure, and the culture of the student. It's worth mentioning the idea of tuning the instrument in a way that's proven to promote spirituality and wellbeing, profound for the artists, performers, and listeners.

Listeners to music at 432 Hz improve spiritually. 432 Hz is clearer than 440 Hz, and more calming. Playing and listening at 432 Hz calms, relaxes, and makes researchers happy. To maximize the emotional impact of their music on listeners, some musicians have even started tuning their instruments to 432 Hz. Nonetheless, scientists and musicians continue to dispute the effects of tuning to this frequency.

Choosing the right method and school for our student is an essential combination. Later, in Chapter 2, we will learn about selecting suitable material based on the student's age and creative health style.

Examination and Review of Various Violin-playing Schools and Teaching Methods

Figure 1: Albert Einstein

"I know that the most joy in my life has come from my violin." *Albert Einstein*

Influenced by his mother, Albert Einstein was a dedicated violinist from an early age. He often played classical music on his violin (that he named 'Lina') as a brainstorming technique.

Abstract

At first, the violin was primarily employed as a musical accompaniment to the dancers and songs, or as a special show. Later on, playing the violin also showed a variety of forms, and became more colorful, and different styles of violin performance-art emerged, owing to changes in the times and technological improvements. This has given rise to the emergence of various violin-playing schools, as mentioned above. There is much literature on the development of violin schools: 17th/18th/19th-century Italian, French or German; 19th/20th- century Russian or Franco-Belgian.

In this first part, we will focus on the analysis and research of these different schools of violin playing and literature, in order to facilitate the future development of the violin-playing art of pedagogy and methodology, to provide some valuable help to the players, and transform them. In Chapter 4 we will recreate these techniques and present them through performance for the twice-exceptional and gifted children, and students with different abilities.

Introduction

The violin was first very popular in Italy. Since the Italian people preferred the violin to all other musical instruments, the Italian School of violin-playing has a long history of development. However, learners in other countries adjusted and improved their Schools too. The performance-art style of each School is individual, and has continuously changed, gradually, over time. Research, and an analysis of the different violin-playing schools, and of the traditional literature, follows.

Italian School

Figure 2: Francesco Maria Veracini (1744)

The Italian violin school is the earliest school in the world in the origin and development of the violin. It was founded in Italian folk violin-playing, and gradually formed its playing style. The School constructed a solid foundation for the future development of the violin-playing art. The founders of the School included people such as Vivaldi, Tartini, and Paganini.

In the 17th century, **Arcangelo Corelli**, an Italian and the country's most famous violinist, known as the 'king of the musicians', was not only a founder of Italian violin-playing, but was also the world's first professional violinist, and played a crucial role in the development of the violin.

Figure 2 (*Italian School*). This image shows the Italian violinist holding his instrument against his chest. This technique is also documented for the Italian violin virtuosi Matteis, Geminiani, Veracini, Locatelli, and others, and was widespread in the Roman social environment long after Corelli's death.

Although a violin held against the chest complicates shifting at first, virtuosi of the time managed the most difficult passages very well with this particular violin technique. While anecdotes report Corelli's failure as a violinist in the highest hand positions, it was certainly not because of this hold, nor was this the reason for the relatively modest technical requirements of Corelli's op. 5. In fact, it is not at all sure that Corelli intended to show his virtuosity with the sonatas of op. 5. Contemporaries applauded Corelli's playing: his skill as a violinist did not lie in the high left-hand positions but rather in his complete control of the bow.

Robert Bremner says that this was a criterion for Corelli's choice of violinists in his orchestras. The ability of Roman orchestras to play with nuanced dynamic control, as described by contemporary observers, confirms this feature of Corelli's violin school.

By the mid-18th century and until the early 19th century, the Italian School had become dominant in most of the countries of Europe. Paganini was the pinnacle of this old Italian tradition. However, Paganini did not affect the 'pedagogical' passing down of violin technique to future generations, unlike Geminiani and the Italian-trained Frideric Handel.

At the time, their conception and execution appeared astonishingly accurate to reality; they could even replicate the screams of cats, and dogs' barking, on their violins, using a range of violin-playing tips, and significantly influencing society at the time. Many performers began to copy their techniques. Corelli then started to arrange and modify some of the junk material left by predecessors, and as a result he developed some relatively regular violin-playing ideas. He'd begun playing the violin as a toddler, and became a professional performer at 13. Paganini was the most distinguished player in the Italian

School. Before the 18th century, the conventional violin-playing style needed to be revised to suit the necessities of society. As the period progressed and changed, people were anxious to experience a new kind of violin playing.

Nicolт Paganini, influenced by the trends at the time, developed his passionate violin-playing technique to express himself in completely his performances, which included playing the violin with much more ideological excitement and free-thinking. His playing style was widely praised then and he was dubbed the 'King of the Violin.' Since then, many well-known performing artists have emerged in the Italian School. As we can see from the overall development, the virtuosos of the Italian School have shown us the singing of the violin by the use of wide and stretching bowings, and have displayed for us the skills of violin playing, the crucial reason why the violin is considered a singing instrument.

Francesco Geminiani

Geminiani's *The Art of Playing on the Violin* emphasized a migration from traditional music to solo and orchestral works.

He felt that the style of music's only representing concrete examples, such as a cuckoo or even dancing styles, was an incorrect one, saying, "The Intention of Music is not only to please the Ear, but to express Sentiments, strike the Imagination, affect the Mind, and command the Passions". One of the most critical of Geminiani's technical instructions was that knowledge of the fingerboard and its geometry was essential for success. Geminiani mapped the tones and semitones found on the violin with the intention that learners would mark their instrument in this way to assist them in their efforts to play in tune.

He also felt that there was one proper position for the left hand: "To Place the first Finger on the first String upon F; the second Finger on the second String upon C; the third Finger on the third String upon G; and the fourth finger correctly on fourth String on D". Practicing this grip will enable students to feel and see the correctly structured left-hand position. The Geminiani Grip, accompanying the Learner's Fingerboard, focused on establishing intonation and posture, and eliminating error. The grip is essential for a beginner's success.

Figure 3: *Geminiani's Learner Fingerboard*

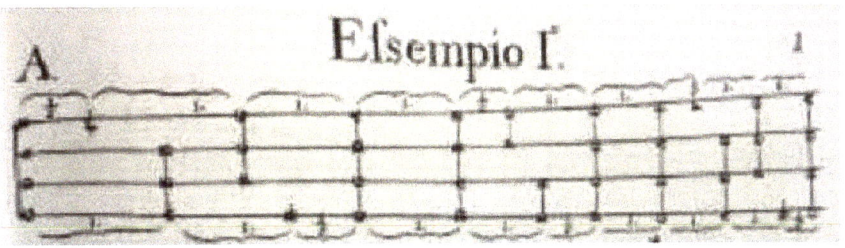

Figure 4: *The Geminiani Grip (Geminiani, n.d.)*

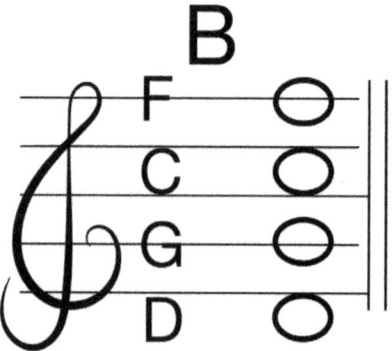

In addition to discussing intonation, Geminiani emphasized tone production. An ideal location exists for holding the bow for maximum sound clarity, and this spot sits a small distance from the frog. He noted that the bow should be held between the thumb and first joint of the fingers and tilted inward. With free, relaxed joints, the player can draw the bow parallel to the bridge with the weight of only the index finger. He felt that the correct tone, the available bows, and musical bow expressions could highlight the violin's beauty. The bow used in Geminiani's time was most likely a Baroque bow, similar to that used by his teacher, Arcangelo Corelli.

The School of Thoughts and Feelings has superseded the Italian School. However, the Italian School continues to play a significant and memorable role in the development of the violin.

Francesco Geminiani

German School

Figure 5: Joseph Joachim (*Wikipedia, n.d.*)

Wolfgang Amadeus Mozart, letter to Leopold Mozart, July 3, 1778

"How popular I would be if I were to lift the German national stage to recognition in music! And this would surely happen for I was already full of desire to write when I heard the German *Singspiel*."[1]

---

1 From *Mozart: the Man and the Artist Revealed in his own Words* (1965), Friedrich Kerst, translated by Henry Krehbiel

The German School also encompasses the Hungarian School, and the style of the German School frequently varied, owing to the Italian School's early influence, and the French School's later influence on the School's development. We should note that the German School's style was shaped by the nation's cultural characteristics, and influenced by various techniques.

Joseph Joachim was a Hungarian violinist. His musical performance seemed more rigorous, an art of tension, and rusticity. It can show the meaning of the works of art, and pays more attention to the emotional expression of the work. He thought that the works of art of a violinist should involve more things: that studying many different art styles, and infusing emotion into performance, is necessary to create a unique art style.

György Ligeti was also a prominent Hungarian representative of the German School during the middle of the 20th century. In his youth, under his father's influence, he attended the Budapest Royal College of Music, and was instructed by Joachim. At 13, Joachim started to perform publicly in the School, which laid a solid foundation for his future career development. He absorbed the influence of many different violin playing styles and gradually formed his unique view with a more precise direction. Through his exceptional abilities, which have significantly contributed to the evolution of the violin, he has provided the public with a wealth of outstanding works.

Literature and Technique

The German School taught a low right arm, and emphasized proper wrist movement in playing. Joachim's pedigree can be traced back to Viotti through Dont, Bohm, and Rode. Joachim and Dont taught Leopold Auer, father of the Russian School, which we will discuss later.

Leopold Mozart was a respected violinist, but he was never significant enough to be an orchestral concertmaster (considered the highest-ranking job of a violinist in his day). Therefore he could have been better known for his violin playing.

However, he was known for his technique, compositions, and book on music criticism (*Fundamental Principles of Violin Playing*). The book's introduction describes the author's frustrations with teaching the improper techniques that students were already trained by, and the difficulties these students encountered after years of playing using substandard methods. He believed that for a student to become a great violinist, the student needed to be knowledgeable. He encouraged studying the string family, followed by the history of music and theory.

Leopold Mozart presented his audience with two options for holding the violin. The first option was to place the tail end of the violin body against the collarbone in a slanted fashion, enabling the bow to be pushed upward instead of back. He claimed that although this position was more "natural looking," it was more "inconvenient" for the player. The second option was the more "comfortable" option. As he explained, the stance was relatively modern: "the violin is placed against the neck so that it lies somewhat in front of the shoulder and the side on which the E (thinnest) string lies under the chin…."

Figure 6: Leopold Mozart holding the violin at his collarbone (first option)

Figure 7: Leopold Mozart holding the violin at his neck (second option)

French School

The rise and influence of the French School is said to have had the effect of diminishing the distinctiveness of other schools, similar to Italy's effect a century earlier.

Figure 8: Rudolf Kreutzer (*Wikipedia, n.d.*)

"Start well & end well. The middle will look after itself." *Stephane Grappelli*

As civilizations progressed, the French School emerged quietly and unobtrusively, and grew increasingly active. To unify French musical art, the Paris Conservatory was officially established in 1795, and formal instruction soon followed. Leo Claire and

Viotti brought the finest elements of the Italian School to France. They fused them with the local culture and art forms, establishing the French School model.

The famous French School representatives are Viotti, Kreutzer, Bayeux, and others.

Giovanni Battista Viotti, a famous Italian violinist and founder of the French School, combined the Italian School's outstanding skills and the French School's performance skills during his long life in Paris. His playing mainly showed us noble momentum and passionate enthusiasm; his performances usually made audiences feel excited and enthusiastic.

Rodolphe Kreutzer was a French violinist and a professor at the Paris Conservatory of Music, with a specific insight into the professional domain. Affected by Viotti, his performance was not only more beautiful, but it also included the specific characteristics of the time.

Literature and Technique

The techniques of the French School incorporated a violinistic technique driven by 'good taste.' Double-stops and harmonics were not often employed. Baillot also gives directions in his treatise for holding the bow, using a straight thumb and straight fingers (*The Art of the Violin*). However, the best model for studying the playing style of the French School would be to study the works by Viotti, Baillot, Kreutzer, and Rode. The four composed more than 70 concerti, and countless other pieces in total.

Kreutzer and Rode wrote étude books. These books provided musical compositions designed as an exercise to improve the technique, or demonstrate the player's skill. Even today, these books help students solidify their technique.

Pierre Baillot, in *The Art of the Violin*, tells how a person should stand and hold the violin, the position of the left and right hand (about the moving parts of the arm), correct bow posture, and the movement of the violinist's fingers while playing. Ultimately, this treatise led to the prominence of the Franco-Belgian method of violin playing.

In previous treatises by others, there had been discussions on how to hold the violin (at the neck, or the collarbone), and the proper method of holding the bow. Baillot also discussed the violinist's body, and the ideal posture when performing on a violin. He began with a list of criteria—almost a checklist—for the student to follow. For example (see below), in his first lesson on how to stand, Baillot provided eleven steps that, once applied, would leave students standing in a way that would benefit their playing.

Figure 9: Baillot—the posture from the front

Drawing by Baillot: Standing Posture
(*The Art of the Violin, Pierre Baillot*)

How to Stand

The body and the head are straight.

The chest is open and forward.

Shoulders back.

The Checklist

1. Practice one thing at a time.

2. Link what the student has just succeeded in doing well with what comes before and after.

3. The less advanced the student, the shorter and more frequent his practice periods should be.

He believed that the metronome, a timing device, should be used "only to learn the composer's initial tempo". He did not wish for the metronome's mechanical, rhythmic pulse to detract from the composer's musical intentions.

Baillot also incorporated the study of compositions into an atypical method of teaching techniques. He believed in a three-step procedure:

1. A definition is provided, along with an illustration to support it.

2. Purely technical exercises are provided, fundamental technical difficulties are summarized; and

3. Finally, an application of all the principles is made to the pieces that are to be chosen

Russian School

Figure 10: Jascha Heifetz (*Wikipedia, n.d.*)

"If I do not practice one day, I know it; two days, the critics know it; three days, the public knows it.
Jascha Heifetz

The Russian School was affected by the impact of the above-described Schools before it came into being. At that time, many artists from Italy, France, and Germany went to Russia for performances which provided a foundation for the formation of the Russian School. The significant representatives of the Russian School include Elman and Heifetz.

Mischa Elman was a Russian-American violinist, and one of the most influential contributors to the development of the Russian School.

In the 20th century, **Jascha Heifetz** was the most accomplished violinist of the Russian School. He had been learning the violin from childhood, and was discovered by the musician Leopold Auer who believed he was a prodigy after hearing him play the violin at the age of six. Thus, Auer personally instructed him at the St. Petersburg Conservatory. His performance was grand and magnificent, achieving a lively and spirited atmosphere. His playing created a loud, expressive sound and he had extraordinary abilities that could convey both the noble and majestic, and the modesty and rigor of romanticism's classics. His performances were always one-of-a-kind, and he could be faithful to the original work, without exaggerated facial expressions.

Literature and Technique

Leopold Auer (1845-1930) is often called the father of the Russian School and its pedagogy.

Many players today refer to the Russian bow hold as an aspect of Auer's Russian School. The characteristics of this bow hold feature the index finger's making contact at the second joint and the whole arm engaging in sweeping motions of the bow.

However, it is essential to note that there were two different Russian schools in the United States. One of Viotti's students, Friedrich Wilhelm Pixis, developed a line of students that led to Sevcik and Stolyarski.

Pyotr Stolyarski formed the second Russian School. He was David Oistrakh's teacher, and he had a remarkable eye for cultivating young students' talent.

Figure 11: Pyotr Stolyarski with a student

Stolyarsky's extraordinary skill as a teacher and organizer, and his incredible determination, enabled him to achieve remarkable results. His method of instruction was grounded in the belief that a child should be prepared for a career in the performing arts from an early age by being exposed to the different creative and professional talents he would need. The child learned to play the violin less 'on' than 'with' it.

American Teachers in the 20th and 21st centuries influenced by the previously described different schools

The most influential teachers in America during the 20th century were Joseph Gingold and Ivan Galamian, followed closely by Dorothy DeLay.

Joseph Gingold was born in Belarus and studied in New York with Graffman (a student of Auer). He then lived in Belgium for several years, studying with Eugene Ysaÿe. He spent several years as the concertmaster of the Cleveland Orchestra, but is best known for his position as a violin professor at Indiana University. Some of his best-known students are Joshua Bell, Joseph Silverstein, and Miriam Fried.

Ivan Galamian was born in Tabriz, Iran, to Armenian parents, and his initial studies were in Moscow with Konstantin Mostras, a student of Auer. He then studied in Paris with Lucien Capet, a descendant of Baillot's teaching and the French School (incidentally, Capet wrote a very enlightening treatise bow use, *Superior Bow Technique*). Galamian taught for several years in Paris, but his eventual and primary position was in

New York, at Juilliard. He has taught countless influential violinists of today, such as Perlman and Zukerman. Perhaps part of the genius of Gingold and Galamian is that they each represented their own 'hybrid school' that employed the best of their varied backgrounds.

When Galamian died, his assistant, Dorothy DeLay, took over his studio at Juilliard. DeLay students abound in the concert halls of America today. Highlights of some of her students are Midori, Perlman, Zukerman, Nigel Kennedy, Gil Shaham, and Sarah Chang.

Figure 12: Dorothy DeLay (*Wikipedia, n.d.*)

"Children become what they are told they are".
Dorothy DeLay

Conclusions

Most violinists nowadays are products of hybrid schools, having had even more diverse influences than Galamian or Gingold. We all learn and are affected by a handful of professors from diverse backgrounds, absorb the best of each, and assimilate them uniquely; thus, few players exhibit distinct School styles.

It is crucial to comprehend the history of the skills and creative legacy passed down, and the wealth of knowledge accumulated, in various geographical regions. Preserving the past, comprehending it, and learning from it are crucial.

In addition to skills, music educators must be well-versed in Music History, Music Theory, Musicology, and Ethnomusicology to bring out the best in their pupils and establish a solid foundation.

What do these Schools and teachings have in common? They recognized the critical necessity for the standardization of violin technique, and played crucial roles in the standardization of the technique. A second commonality is that the authors (the ancestors of violin schools) did not develop a permanent technique. They could observe and record, which allowed their written theories to conform to the prevalent practices of the time. Due to changes in the violin, bow, and compositional demands, playing technique has continued to evolve throughout history. The theory follows the practice: although contemporary music and performance methods have moved beyond their origins, they remain a firm foundation for our present and future pupils.

On Composers, analyzing, and application

How we analyze music is how we let ourselves influence it.

It is essential that we learn about the composer's life and history, his creative health style, and the why, the what, and the how of the musical creation. We can define ourselves by the symphony; or take motivation from it, and use it to craft our own symphony. There is a simple psychology here that is powerful: but as Confucius once said, "Everything has beauty, but not everyone can see it".

Choosing the right musical piece or symphony can change our life's direction, and, if used correctly, serve as motivating tool, emotional support, and friendship. It can be our friend if we tend to be introverts. It can protect us if we have experienced trauma and are unaware. By using a composer who had the same childhood experience, his music can be our teacher, therapist, mood stabilizer, dopamine, and serotonin.

In one of my research papers below, I was trying to find meaning (it was like a puzzle), and to discover the depth which is the soul of The Theory of Music, Nutrition, the Environment, and their influence.

"I am part of a light, and it is the music. The Light fills my six senses: I see it, hear, feel, smell, touch, and think. Thinking of it means my sixth sense. Particles of

Light are written notes. A bolt of lightning can be an entire sonata. A thousand balls of lightning is a concert... For this concert, I have created a Ball Lightning, which can be heard on the icy peaks of the Himalayas." (Nicola Tesla)

As Tesla wrote, light fills his six senses, and he can see it, hear, feel, smell, touch, and think it. I believe that the power of foods and festive, bright, light music, with spring water sounds, and the correct dose of green tea, can be transformative, and an instrument to unblock, smooth, and assist every student, no matter their age or profession, when fighting to clear a block inside the mind. Sometimes it is difficult to push ourselves, but as Einstein once said: "Life is like riding a bicycle. To keep our balance, we must keep moving".

So let us do a brief analysis.

The Theory of Music

Beethoven's Influence on my Life through the Ninth Symphony

Introduction

The purpose of this essay is to describe the influence of classical music on our personal lives, and how its notes overflow as a watercolor that is depicted through our being, through our thoughts. We become the composition, and as a painting we are exhibited, presented to others, who perhaps will not understand us, understand our personality, or accept our character. And a 'miracle' might happen, with some exceptional person who will accept us, and understand us the way the marvelous story of the great composers has drawn us.

The great composers have, like the most enchanting poem, poured their notes, their every moment, into the most magnificent compositions—such as Beethoven's Ninth Symphony, which will forever remain in the history of music as one of the most powerful, mysterious, and profound works. Works that have not only painted our lives, but have affixed their seal upon the universe, thus leaving music infinite and unrivaled among all its phenomena.

"Music represents power; she has the power to wake up all our senses as she is the cure for our soul. Thanks to her, all sounds become terms. A sound is not just a sound anymore, but a word, a music sentence of which are born the biggest works and interpretations by the biggest artists and composers." (My Personal Statement, October 2013)

In this analysis, we will focus on Beethoven's Ninth Symphony—on what an impact it had on my life and personality, and what it represented to me through different situations and emotions that I have encountered during all these years of growing up and playing. We will not neglect Beethoven's life, and how he felt, with his quotes upholding this theory that we are analyzing—my theory.

We will cover all four movements, and compare them with my movements (my character, mind, soul, and peace). We'll pay close attention to the fourth movement, *Ode to Joy*, for with it he has changed the views of many nations, and sent very important and positive messages, leading it to become a hymn of Europe in 1947.

Once these facts and analyses are observed and understood, the real essence of the impact of Symphony No. 9 will come to light.

A Description of the Ninth Symphony's Creation, and its Premiere

Symphony No. 9 in D minor, Op. 125 (known as *The Choral*), is the final completed symphony of Ludwig van Beethoven (1770-1827). Completed in 1824, despite criticism it remains listed as one of the most brilliant and grandiose symphonies; and according to some, one of the greatest musical works ever written.

On November 10, 1822, the directors of the Philharmonic Society of London decided to offer Beethoven

£50 for a manuscript Symphony. On November 15, he received the offer; and on December 20th he accepted, and had been given permission to deliver it at the end of nine months. The work turned out to be Beethoven's Ninth Symphony: but he failed to comply with the deadline, and not even the directors of the Philharmonic Society saw anything until 1824. Despite the fact that Beethoven was happy to agree to all the terms of the commission from the beginning, he allowed the symphony to have its first performance in Vienna on May 7, 1824 at the Karntnertor-Theater—preventing the premiere from taking place in London as agreed.

The first performance in London was on March 21st, 1825, at the Argyll Rooms in Regent Street. It was described as a "New Grand Characteristic Sinfonia with Vocal Finale" and was conducted by Sir George Smart, one of the founding members of the Philharmonic Society. "The Performance was not all that Smart could have hoped for and the audience was more confused than adulatory" (Peter Avis, 1999). It was 20 years before the company performed their £50 Symphony again.

An interesting snippet is that from March 30th to May 4th, Ludwig Rellstab (a Berlin music critic, 1799-1860) visited Vienna, heard the Ninth Symphony, and called on Beethoven more than once (*Beethoven and His World: A Biographical Dictionary* by H. P. Clive). Rellstab also gave its name to the *Moonlight* sonata, after Beethoven's death.

In addition… The first part of the beginning:

"To you, brother Carl,

I give special thanks for the attachment you have shown me of late. It is my wish that you may have a better and freer life than I have

had. Recommend virtue to your children; it alone, not money, can make them happy. I speak from experience." Ludwig Van Beethoven (Heiligenstadt Testament, October 6, 1802).[2]

And it all began with…

Although I was only 5 years old, I had a feeling that I was caught between two times: the end of the eighteenth/beginning of the nineteenth century, and the period where I was at that moment—at the end of the 20th century and on the threshold of the 21st. I felt and dreamed that I was part of the period of late romanticism and classicism; I wanted to live in that time, to play, to create… Later on,

---

2 Quote taken from Munteanu, I. 2004-14. Heiligenstadt Testament (October 6, 1802) to his brothers. Retrieved from http://www.all-about-beethoven.com/heiligenstadt_test.html

when I learned to read, I consumed the books of Jane Austin, Charles Dickens...

In my time...

One day, my mother took me for a walk, to buy me a dress for my first day in kindergarten. I was almost six years old. Passing by a clothing shop, I saw a music store nearby, and I stopped in front of it. In the window were the tapes of all my favorite classical composers. I could not resist: I knew I had to pick out the tape with classical music that would be my best friend:

Beethoven's Symphony No. 9[3] was the tape that I chose. And together with it, my journey to music began. The four movements of the symphony are:

Allegro ma non troppo, un poco maestoso;

Scherzo: Molto vivace–Presto;

Adagio molto e cantabile–Andante Moderato–Tempo Primo–Andante Moderato–Adagio–Lo Stesso Tempo; and the fourth movement: *Presto; Allegro molto assai (Alla marcia); Andante maestoso; Allegro energico, sempre ben marcato*

---

3   My tape, Beethoven's Symphony No.9, recorded by Mister Records Ltd.

They were identical to:

My personality and character; my sadness and hope; my spirit and inner peace; and finally, my soul, mind, heart, and dreams.

His Symphony had an impact on my life: I grew up with it. It was my shield, my comfort when I felt blue, and the moving force for all my achieved dreams so far.

Of course, I did not stop there. Although my parents were not musicians, they enjoyed classical music. When I was in first grade, at the age of seven, my choral singing and music teacher noticed that I stood apart from my peers: I had a special respect and great

love for classical music, and was the only one who could sing *Ode to Joy*. One day, after a school class, my teacher took me to a special music school, where I met the director, and they immediately organized my audition. One of the professors at the audition wanted to see my fingers, and told me I should play the violin. And it became reality. In the morning I would go to the elementary school, and in the evening I had lessons at the music school.

It was time for my first concert, at which I played Beethoven's Minuet; and I slowly started to find out about many of his other works–his Violin Romance No.2 in F Major, his Violin Concerto in D Major...

which also had a further impact on my life, and guided me through many everyday situations while I was a teenager.

As I grew up and started playing the viola and piano at a music school, I became friends with Beethoven's *Pathetique Sonata, The Tempest...* But the most valued, and the other half of me that complemented me, made me brave, a fighter, was Beethoven's Symphony No. 9.

Whenever I felt sad and without motivation, I would recall the words of my friend, composer, and idol, Beethoven:

> "But what a humiliation for me when someone standing next to me heard a flute in the distance and I heard nothing, or someone heard a shepherd singing and again I heard nothing. Such incidents drove me almost to despair; a little more of that and I would have ended my life - it was only my art that held me back." (Heiligenstadt Testament, October 6, 1802)[4]

Beethoven, who, in the worst mood, full of sorrow, without will, with the thought that no one under-

---

4   Quote taken from Munteanu, I. 2004-14. *Heiligenstadt Testament* (October 6, 1802) to his brothers. Retrieved from http://www.all-about-beethoven.com/heiligenstadt_test.html

stood him and sympathized with him, wrote the most fascinating work: his Symphony No. 9, which to this day is one of the most beautiful things that has ever happened to humanity, and whose orchestration and notes unite many people, present peace, dignify, and know no boundaries. And although in one of his conversations with Brentano, he stated that

> "Music is the one incorporeal entrance into the higher world of knowledge which comprehends mankind, but which mankind cannot comprehend." (W. N. Sullivan, Beethoven: His Spiritual Development (Alfred A. Knopf, 1927), pp. 3-4.)[5],

I think that with his last symphony, mankind became more aware, richer in spiritual values, and as in the fourth movement, filled with joy.

---

5   Quote taken from Sullivan, J.W.N. (1936). *Beethoven - His Spiritual Development*. New York: Alfred A. Knopf. Retrieved from https://archive.org/details/beethovenhisspir002615mbp.

My Analysis

First movement:

Allegro ma non troppo, un poco maestoso or: my personality and character. A movement that depicts the revolutionary spirit, longing for freedom, escape from everyday life. Listening to the first movement, I knew it was me. I was only 12 years old, and it was my temple when I thought my parents did not understand me. I did not feel alone, and had no need to tell anyone how I felt, for there was my guardian angel—the sound that protected me and gave me full support. In the beginning, in the first two minutes of listening, I had the feeling that I'd received the best advice from the notes: the advice that taught me to be patient, but not to lose my sense of independence.

When I enrolled at the High School of Music, I often felt disappointed by unfair situations. Whether it was about a concert, or competition, the privileges always went to children whose parents were professors: but I did not give up. I was persistent, and kept practicing the viola even more, mentally and physically. I felt no pressure: all my interest in music, all my will and support for practicing was springing from me, and from Beethoven's music.

Second movement:

The second movement of Beethoven's Ninth Symphony—*Scherzo: Molto vivace–Presto*—stirred further my confidence and motivation. Whenever I was seeking a solution to a problem, I got the answer from this movement. I always had to fight for everything alone; at home I never felt accepted the way I wished to be. I was the only artist in the family, different from everybody. Musicians are always more sensitive, and sometimes they also need Melancholy in the role of muse to serve them as inspiration…

But the incredibly joyous *Scherzo*, originally intended for *fugato*, the idea of which he did not abandon, the general form of which conveys indescribable joy of such intensity and depth, until the *Scherzo* overshadows it like the sunset… In me it awakens motivation—accompanied with confidence.

Third movement:

Then in the third movement—*Adagio molto e cantabile*—appeared the first feeling of falling in love, a new atmosphere different from the previous movements. A new cycle of the sincerest lyrical moments, which rejects any sadness, doubt, and misunderstanding. The first melody comes as gradually designing the chorales of a melodic performance, rarefied on the side by the chords of the instruments, and then a melody accompanied by a secondary theme in a different structure, which paints a picture of the moon and the sun dancing until the end of the infinity of their love.

This movement to me has always represented 'Peace and Tranquility'. Music was my first love, and this movement, from the first moment I took the tape and let the Ninth Symphony play powerfully through the course of my childhood, suggested that, and one day it confirmed it. That was the moment when I enrolled at the Faculty of Music, and I decided that I wanted to play my own life. I was the instrument that interpreted my life through my playing the compositions of the great composers like Beethoven, Brahms, Walton...

Beethoven's Symphony No. 9 is his last symphony, and he is the first composer to have imported voices into a symphony, verses taken from the poem *Ode to Joy* by Friedrich Schiller in the...

Fourth movement:

Although it was very sad, and struggled to finish unwillingly, each phrase of the fourth movement gave one positive thought, like a prayer. It did not lose hope, carrying the power of God within itself. With the baritone verses of the fourth movement of the recitative,

"Oh Friends, not these sounds, but let us strike more agreeable and joyous ones!" Beethoven wanted to show the powerful tones of the human voice; he yearned for a sound filled with soul in the orchestration of all his movements.

The outstanding Beethoven was not trying to touch the words, but to get an even bigger, more spiritual, noble, and charming sound, not because of the structure of the symphony, but because of the sound that was the sincerest, and filled with happiness, to be felt in the air.

The music historian Paul Lang says of Beethoven that "there is still no department of music that does not owe him its very soul."

That movement: *Presto; Allegro molto assai (Alla marcia); Andante maestoso; Allegro energico, sempre ben marcato*, the sound that finally celebrates its freedom and rejoices in its realized dreams, the notes that erase every sorrow, all anger and pain, and create Spring, with the harmonious voice of birds (*Ode to Joy*)… As I listened to it continuously, optimism was created in me: I began to create big dreams, and the longing to contribute even more to those who need help the most was born in me. So I started to perform in charity concerts and projects that helped children without parents. Although they did not know about classical music, they accepted it as if they had been listening to it from birth.

Conclusion

"What you are, you are by accident of birth; what I am, I am by myself. There are and will be a thousand princes; there is only one Beethoven." (Ludwig van Beethoven)

Music can reach and have influence on many people, in different ways. I understand that with new generations come new tastes in music: but for me, classics will always remain in first place. Classical music, and especially the Ninth Symphony, have led me through life. I began to discover and reveal even more meaning in music, as I've mentioned before. I became an independent and courageous individual, without any fear that a dream would not be achieved. Whatever I wanted, with music I had it all. It was, and still is, my best friend; it made me strive to be even better in my profession as a musician, accompanying me on many international competitions and master-class workshops in the period between moving from high school to university, which resulted in huge results. When I was 20 years old, I'd already played in the orchestra of the Macedonian Opera and Ballet. I took part in competitions where I won two international and one national award. It brought me many concerts and collaborations with musicians from Slovenia, Japan, and Germany. In 2008, I worked on two humanitarian projects, and received an award in acknowledgement of these from the city where I live.

I was the first classical musician to carry out these projects. However, my desire to help people, using the talent that the Lord gave me, and to do even more, did not stop—and never will. The last award that I received, the *Feniks*, concerned "achievements in the music culture and the arts"… It is that universal language of music, and the passion for life, the gift that the great composers of classical music have given us.

P.S. Thank you, Beethoven, for the wonderful Ninth Symphony and all your other works, which have left a positive mark on me—on my childhood, and now, and into the future.

Yours faithfully,

Sofija

"At a certain place in Beethoven's Ninth Symphony, for example, he might feel that he is floating above the earth in a starry dome, with the dream of immortality in his heart; all the stars seem to glimmer around him, and the earth seems to sink ever deeper downwards." (Fredrick Nietzsche, *Human, All too Human*)[6]

---

6   Retrieved from: http://www.brainyquote.com/quotes/authors/l/ludwig_van_beethoven

The Theory of Nutrition

The Concept of Diet and Its Impact on the Environment

Now that we've covered music, let's talk about food. Isn't it great to have something healthy and enjoyable to eat? I'm referring to the darker varieties of chocolate—the kind that our mothers have always used in the kitchen! Pure serotonin is a chemical that can alter one's mood, and is the basis for the operation of many medications. Dark chocolate raises serotonin levels in the brain, and stimulates the production of serotonin in the intestines; as a result of all these effects, it can assist with the functioning of our immune system. The Mayans of Central America are credited with creating the first documented records of chocolate consumption. The Mayans "not only consumed chocolate but revered it." The flavoring component known as tyramine can be found in chocolate, derived from the amino acid tyrosine. The development of dopamine begins with the amino acid tyrosine. When there is a rise in tyrosine levels, there is also a rise in dopamine levels. This rise in dopamine levels activates the reward center that is located in the brain. This dopamine pathway may also help explain the pleasure experienced after tasting, and the mood improvement it brings about.

The consumption of green tea has been documented for more than two thousand years, showing it to be the second most popular beverage in the world. This tea is loaded with various bioactive compounds which have been shown to benefit multiple diseases, including depression.

The consumption of green tea can assist in the alleviation of oxidative stress which is a COMT inhibitor, a naturally occurring enzyme in our brains that degrades several motivational neurotransmitters, including dopamine, norepinephrine, and epinephrine. Drinking green tea can increase your body's levels of dopamine. It is important to note that it should only be consumed in the appropriate quantity, which I will discuss later.

When I first started giving private lessons on the violin and piano, I told my students to brew a cup of green tea whenever they needed either a boost of energy while practicing on a musical instrument, or inspiration to get started on practicing at home. In terms of mental performance, it works mental miracles.

Doing Something Physical

According to some researchers, reading ability can also be improved by exposure to the color green; therefore, if we do not wish to read, why don't we go for a 20-minute walk, followed by ten minutes of staring at the green grass? Discipline, repetition, and timing are more important than anything else. According to Panteleimon Ekkekakis, Ph.D., a professor of kinesiology at Iowa State University, regular exercise causes the same structural changes in the brain that are thought to be behind the effectiveness of antidepressant medication. These changes are considered to be behind the fact that the drug can treat depression. These changes are produced by physical activity, which has side effects such as improved mood, weight control, and cardiovascular health. However, according to my research findings, when combined with nutrition, consistently and simultaneously every day, exercise can move us forward from a point where we believe it is difficult and impossible to get out.

How exactly does getting some exercise help those who are depressed or anxious?

By releasing feel-good endorphins.

By taking your mind off your problems and worries.

By helping you to gain confidence.

By helping you to participate in more social activities.

By maintaining your health.

This is the guidance that I share with my students. Occasionally, I will place a sheet of green see-through paper on top of what I am reading.

Musical content helps to increase our reading speed, as well as our level of comprehension.

My Research Diet consists of the different theories listed earlier.

Maintaining a consistent schedule for eating, going to bed, and engaging in physical activity every day is essential. I spent a total of two weeks conducting this research. When I started, I felt down, unable to muster any motivation, exhausted, and blocked.

You should always go to bed before midnight. (It is important never to go beyond midnight, as you will always feel tired in the morning, no matter how many hours you have slept.)

Three cups of green tea before 7 p.m. (Three cups are sufficient, because it contains the same amount of caffeine as one cup of coffee. But on the other hand, green tea releases those necessary chemicals to motivate our brain in order to begin an action or activity.)

If we were to drink more cups, it could serve as an effective sedative; however, this would be the case only when we were anxious.

At 7 o'clock, I run at my usual pace for twenty minutes while listening to Beethoven's Ninth Symphony, and then I sit in the park and stare at the grass for ten minutes while I do nothing but think how green it is.

Listening to music: (what will happen is that memories from your childhood will start coming back to you, and you will start feeling the longing to strive to continue with your dream.)

A cup of hot cocoa an hour and a half before going to bed: (it releases serotonin, helps positive thinking, and stops the worries which result in insomnia).

AFTER TWO WEEKS, THESE ARE THE RESULTS:

I started feeling motivated, light, energized, and consistent, with the urge to continue doing what I'd done for two weeks—without trying hard, or thinking about doing it. I felt eager to continue working on my music projects, and to complete the tasks that I had been putting off.

I was not depressed, so I started watching comedies, which made me laugh; I did not want to be depressed.

It was when I started loving myself, and visualizing myself as a child, that the change happened. I remembered how I played with flowers, picking leaves from the chamomile to make tea with my mom, and picking the Denim 'n Lace Russian Sage to make a headband, making a hole in the green stalk and putting the other flowers through this. My mother would then put it on my head. And so I rediscovered my interest in life.

I had the impression that nothing could hold me back. Time is a Valuable Resource. Additionally..............

When everything is considered:

We need additional research to develop a better mind-set for maintaining consistency and discipline in our mental and overall wellness. Addressing this issue at an earlier age, in childhood, and teaching our children to appreciate nature, would help them to help themselves without the need for medication. It can be of great benefit for our health and well-being, and help us cope with challenging tasks. It can open our minds to new ways of learning how to live. We can also find new music, and analyze it for individuals suffering from mood and anxiety disorders, to help them move forward.

With our varied temperaments, with our different abilities, we need to learn to waltz with them, rather than attempting to eradicate them with medication as we mature into adults.

The objective of this paper was to illustrate the impact that classical music has on our private lives, environment, and nutrition, and to show how music's notes overflow like a watercolor that is depicted through our being and our thoughts. We are exhibited and presented to others, who may or may not understand us and our personality, or accept our character, our theories and our goals. The impact of music can become for us the same as Beethoven's Ninth Symphony, which will forever remain in the history of music as one of the most powerful, mysterious, and profound works. It has not only painted our lives, but has also affixed its seal in the universe, thereby leaving music infinite and unrivaled in all its incarnations.

Table 3

The effects of tea against CVDs based on clinical studies.

Subjects	Substances	Treatments	Effects and Mechanisms	Ref.
155 healthy participants	A green tea containing O-methylated catechin	12 g/d for 12 weeks	LDL-C↓, LAB↓	[85]
151 participants aged 30–70 y	Green tea	1.8 g/d for 12 weeks	LDL-C↓	[86]
15 participants aged 18–35 y and 15 participants aged 55–75 y	Green tea	2 cups/d for 14 days	Improving SBP and skin microvascular function	[89]
20 women aged 32.7–49.5 y	Green tea extract	500 mg for 4 weeks	SBP↓	[90]
50 healthy men	Green tea	A single dose of 200 mg EGCG	Improving flow-mediated dilation	[94]
14 healthy individuals	Green tea polyphenol-enriched ice cream	A single dose of 100 g	Oxidative stress↓, Vascular function↑	[95]
79 hypertension patients aged 20–55 y	Flavonoids from green tea	425.8 ± 13.9 mg epicatechin equivalents for 6 months	SBP↓, DBP↓	[91]
60 individuals with mild hypercholesterolemia	Catechin-enriched green or oolong tea	780.6 mg/d or 640.4 mg/d catechin for 12 weeks	TC↓, LDL-C↓, TG↓	[87]
1075 healthy postmenopausal women	Catechins	1315 mg for 1 year	TC↓, LDL-C↓, non-HDL-C levels↓	[26]
99 participants aged 25–60 y with mild hypercholesterolemia	Phytosterol-enriched instant black tea	2.5 g/d for 4 weeks	Blood lipids↓	[88]

Open in a separate window

Figure 13: The effects of tea

Keeping a healthy, creative brain by employing musical composition as a method of treatment

I was financially self-sufficient, and able to fund my education. As a first-generation student, I remember being overjoyed at having my dream job, and the opportunity to attend college. When I was 18, I started working as a viola tutti in the Orchestra and Ballet. When I started, the first piece in my repertoire was Tchaikovsky's *Swan Lake,* and I was young and eager. Nonetheless, I gradually began to feel that I couldn't grow and learn in the workplace, or build a career, because of the culture and hierarchy in the country where I was born. So I decided to go to university in London, having received a scholarship for my postgraduate studies. I soon had to return home and continue performing for the theatre. The College in London kept my scholarship, but I did not return to study, because I couldn't financially support my living there. It was difficult for international students to secure the living fees, because of the law standards in my country. But when we really want something, as Paulo Coelho said, the universe conspires for us to have it.

I was given another chance. I received a letter inviting me to study at the Conservatory Liceu in Barcelona, and an email from a teacher at the Boston Conservatory, who wanted to have me in her studio. I debated what to do. London awaited me: possibilities were one distant location, and two European schools. When I was about to discuss studying in Spain with my father, he purchased a ticket to America for me.

I came to Boston and had to apply for student jobs at the university because that was the only way I could pay my rent. Moreover, I had four jobs. I was a wellness assistant, marketing assistant, concert services student worker, and I recorded concerts as a video assistant in the AV department. At one point I needed to secure money for the next year, so I had to go back to London, where I worked at a pizza restaurant, because as an international student I was not allowed to work in the USA. I had to finish, and I wanted to make this happen because I'd paused my studies in London. "This time!" I promised; and I did it, again with the help of music, and the sun that shines in Boston in the winter, unlike the rain in London.

As soon as I'd started my studies in Boston, in the second semester I decided to work on a project. Since I had a student job at the health and wellness office, I decided to create a project, propose it to my supervisor, and connect with the Music Therapy department at Berklee College, in Boston. The project was called "Honoring the Mind of the Artist". I invited some musicians, friends, and students, and asked them if they wanted to perform and talk about their anxiety or stage-fright, or anything else, while they performed a piece by the particular composer that they were studying. They could learn how that composer coped at a time where there was no medication, only music.

To do my project successfully, and be inspired to find a music 'medicine' to heal others, I started learning about and researching the composers who'd experienced different brain creativity—such as bi-polar disorder, depression, melancholy, and others. Inspired by all these composers and their creative health, I decided to design a one-off program offering students an opportunity to perform the music of composers who'd faced creative health challenges, at the same time sharing their experiences in a safe environment, managing stage-fright, and coping with depression and anxiety. It was a part of my graduate project, but it was constructive, and I showed that it could work. It was effective immediately: once we discuss, accept, and embrace our vulnerability, and share how it inspired us to create, we are winners. This is contrary to what we are expected to be at universities: we have to keep an excellent profile, and satisfy the public image, though inside we burn out slowly.

My adventure of delving more deeply into investigating and evaluating the composers of the 19th century (and later) began at this point, and continued from there.

Let us explore this research, looking at what I found out about them, trying to help others by accepting who we are, and learning to discuss any anxiety or different brain creativity over a cup of tea, as the composers from the Renaissance and up to the 20th century did.

The Composers and their Creative Health Style (Research Paper)

Introduction

During the last five hundred years, the typical lifespan of a composer has been longer than sixty years. All composers who suffered from anxiety and depression had their pathologies and diagnoses described.

I chose composers from various eras, cultures, and ethnicities to demonstrate that mental health issues are universal, and affect people from all walks of life. This could be used by us as a tool, by applying their composition to someone else's condition; or it could make us feel better by knowing that the great composers experienced and accepted themselves while suffering what we might encounter, or are going through. This contributes to our own development as artists and professionals.

Purposefully, I chose different composers from different countries worldwide, from Europe and America, to demonstrate the wide range of global musical styles and influences that exist. This approach allowed me to showcase the diversity of music, the richness of the genre, and its ability to transcend cultural boundaries. Creative brain health exists everywhere, connecting all of these composers. If only the world could have accepted their individuality, the uniqueness of their brain creativity, and treated it as a gift instead of a weakness. These days, the same gifted talents are still alive and thriving: composers, artists, writers, poets, all of them—and the ones that are still to be born. The younger generations' creative brains would not burn out so quickly if they were better understood and better treated: they would continue building and expanding their creativity, which gushes like a waterfall, and which contributes to the further development of new ideas, helping everyone in need.

Wolfgang Amadeus Mozart (1756-1791)

Mozart was an Austrian composer, pianist, and conductor. Amadeus was not a handsome man. He was sensitive to comments about his looks; his psyche was complex, and somewhat impressive. Mozart was a man of high intelligence and showed the capacity for extraordinarily imaginative creativity and original thought. Also, he was able to put great effort into everything he did. His inflated inner image of himself sometimes led him to excessive narcissism, exhibitionism, and arrogance. This created many enemies throughout his life.

He showed a particular trait of dependence and was compliant and submissive to his father's will. He was spontaneously generous, which made him easy prey for hangers-on. He used to suffer in silence. His way of dealing with aggression was passive and self-destructive.

Mozart suffered from a condition that could be called a cyclothymic disorder. There is some evidence that his mother suffered from the same condition. His hypomanic episodes were characterized by elevated mood, excessive energy, inflated self-esteem, increased productivity, physical hyperactivity, and inappropriate behavior, with no sense of the likely outcome. Sometimes he wrote nonsense in his letters. Techniques used in those letters include paraphrases, anagrams, and foolish rhymes and verses. Sometimes he would behave with deliberate, self-demeaning clowning. His economics seemed to be part of his hypomanic syndrome, leading to serious financial troubles.

His depression got worse after his father's death. Depressive spells would develop after hypomanic swings.

Sometimes these depressive and hypomanic symptoms alternated rapidly, within a day, or even an hour. In his depressive phases, he was highly irritable, melancholic, apathetic, and dominated by imagination. He would suffer insomnia, and a tendency to paranoia, jealousy, exhaustion, and fatigue.

There are at least two essential elements of Mozart's cyclothymic disorder that could have significantly contributed to shortening his life. First is his workoholism, a fatal habit for a genius who cared nothing for his health, and kept exhausting himself by working. Second is his alcoholism, which might be called symptomatic. He may have suffered some predilection, partly owing to fever during his terminal illness. Mozart's friend, Schikanaeder,[7] and his group pushed Mozart to excessive drinking, through which he could briefly escape life's reality, and no doubt alleviate the symptoms of depression and somatic disease, and even hangovers.

Owing to his temper and character, Mozart led a reckless life and worked obsessively to the point of complete exhaustion. He drank alcohol (especially punch) throughout his life. Even before his symptomatic alcoholism mentioned earlier (under the influence of

---

7   Emanuel Schikaneder was more than just a patron of the opera, as well as a cast member: he wrote the libretto of the Magic Flute, and he and Mozart were personal friends.

Schikanaeder's group), he suffered from semi-conscious states and mild epileptic seizures. His neurasthenia could have been a common expression of his artistic personality.

Ludwig van Beethoven (1770-1827)

Beethoven was a German composer, pianist, and conductor, born into a family of musicians.

In about 1800, his musical career was seriously jeopardized when he slowly started losing his hearing. Unable to accept his illness, he lived a miserable, solitary life, trying to keep his deafness secret. Ludwig wished for more compassion and understanding among people, particularly women. He did not have any permanent relationship with a woman: he would not believe

that women appreciated the company of the famous musician, even though he was short, and had an average appearance. Feeling this shattered Beethoven's heart.

Therefore, as early as 1802, he wrote the *Heiligenstadt Will*, describing his health problems and his complete despair. Nevertheless, fortunately he decided not to give up. Hand in hand with his health issues, Ludwig experienced a severe professional crisis, which resulted in lower musical productivity.

Although his popularity was growing, the progressive loss of his hearing made him unable to perform as well as before, either as a pianist or a conductor. Very quickly, this started to affect his career, because Beethoven failed to maintain the public's interest. With his uncontrollable and violent temper, he had to change his residence often. He was rude and distrustful toward his landladies, doctors, acquaintances, and friends. He led a solitary, emotionally intense life. In a way, this contributed to his musical creativity.

For more than 30 years he had been misusing alcohol, hoping to escape the severe depression he had fallen into because of his deafness and other illnesses. He used to drink about 100 grams of absolute alcohol daily, and usually 1 liter of wine. Buyers of his music would bribe him with bottles of his preferred wines. He was a regular customer at local inns, usually drinking champagne, punch, and beer. He was not pleasant company when he was drunk. The opinion is that even a smaller quantity of alcohol than previously mentioned could cause severe liver damage. Beethoven's alcoholism was also evident in his swollen face. He completely disregarded doctors' advice to avoid alcohol: on the contrary, he drank even more, unable to control himself.

Robert Schumann (1810-1856)

Schumann was a German composer, pianist, and conductor.

The Schumann family was a family of intellectuals, and very sensible individuals; but his family had some psychiatric diseases, like schizophrenia and depression, which occasionally ended with hospitalization or suicide.

Schumann's childhood was shadowed by his mother's long illness, because of which she neglected to raise her children properly. He was a compassionate and anxious child, sometimes depressive, and with a sleeping disorder.

Alcohol harmed his physical and mental health; he experienced great fear, developed a personality disorder, and hallucinated. His imagination broadened under the influence of black coffee and nicotine. Schumann described his hallucinations as dreaming awake, sometimes with hearing hallucinations. He experienced depressive and hypochondriacal phases.

In his diary he wrote about the sounds in his ears, complaining that they bothered him, and seriously thinking about committing suicide. He also noted a difference between creative guzzling and drunkenness (unfortunately, the last-mentioned was one of his major problems). On the other hand, guzzling helped him in his creative work.

The year when he turned 23 brought him a lot of excitement, alcohol excess, and stress. He was shocked by the death of his brother's wife, and showed pre-psychotic signs.

Although Schumann drank a lot to get over his neurosis and schizoid tendencies more quickly, he hallucinated and "light-seeing" states, and heard music inside his head.

In his fortieth year, Robert transformed. He shut down emotionally and socially, struggled as a conductor, and fought with the orchestra until they played only his works.

As time went on, he lost some of his inventiveness. When he was 44 he began writing about his telepathic bond with Brahms. He read hidden messages within the lines of letters. His sanity finally broke when he began having excruciating night-time sound encounters, involving tone A. Every sound was like a musical instrument amplifying a whisper in his mind.

These experiences became increasingly unpleasant, and he felt that music had turned into terrifying presences hounding him. He screamed in pain, and became violent to his wife and children. He even saw Schubert's figure, allegedly being sent a beautiful melody by him.

Full of fear and frustration, escaping from home in 1854, Schumann tried to drown himself by jumping into the river Rhine: but a fishermen pulled him out of the water against his will. After that suicide attempt, feeling depressed, and worrying about his aggression toward his family, Schumann demanded to be institutionalized.

He spent the last two years of his life in a sanatorium, Endenich, near Bonn/Rh (30 miles from his home). He was given special care and respect because of his celebrity status. He had several rooms, and lived in great comfort, but had only a few friends to talk to, especially from the same social class. Dr Richarz, who ran the sanatorium, made a great effort to treat patients well. Schumann's condition, with only a few pauses, worsened continuously.

The cause of his relatively early death could be the stimulative psychoactive remedies that Schumann was continuously taking: alcohol in the first place, and coffee, tobacco, and drugs. As an analgesic therapy, and for psychological reasons, he was taking an opium derivate—laudanum.

Robert Schumann's psychiatric condition concerned his doctors. Severe attacks of depression and hypomania, and psychotic states of schizophrenic origin, alternated during his lifetime, with alcohol and other psychoactive substances misused as "auto therapy."

Claude Debussy (1862-1918)

Debussy was a French composer. Women seemed drawn to him even though he was not physically handsome. As he was very sensitive, and emotionally insecure, this helped him improve his low self-esteem.

At the age of 43, Debussy started to experience physical and mental exhaustion. He sought comfort in various sedatives, and even problematic drugs, to ease the emotional emptiness. He turned into a person with a very complex personality—self-centered and antisocial.

This was the attempt of a desperate man to find comfort and fulfillment, as well as inspiration for composing.

Bela Bartok (1881-1945)

He was a Hungarian composer. He was graceful, of medium height, and had brown eyes. He was rather far-sighted (often wearing glasses), and his hair turned grey early. He was nervous, hypersensitive, and constantly dissatisfied with what he had done, always craving something better (the trait of many researchers). A schizoid character, he was often melancholic and depressive.

Edvard (Hagerup) Grieg (1843-1907)

Grieg was a Norwegian composer, conductor, and pianist. He got tuberculosis on his left side in 1859.

He was a compassionate, neurotic man, hospitalized multiple times. He knew that his songs mirrored his vulnerability.

During the last three years of his life, especially in the final year, he became increasingly nervous, weak, and depressed, saying goodbye to his friends forever, aware of the nearness of his death.

Gioacchino Rossini (1792-1868)

An Italian composer. He did not compose anything after the age of 37, for the next 30 years. The success of his earlier life, and exhaustion, caused this inactivity: Rossini had financial security guaranteed for as long as he lived, with a large pension and other benefits.

He suffered from lumbago, with expressive-depressive moods and general nervous exhaustion. He began periodical spa therapy; but maybe that was his escape from other people's company. Everything led to his tiredness and general decline in expression: spiritual sadness, social isolation, and lack of creativity.

He was distraught at his father's death, although his father died when he was very old.

Jean-Jacques Rousseau (1712-1778)

Jean-Jacques was a French philosopher, publicist, and composer of Swiss descent. He lived in poverty, and was often ill. He was restless, incoherent, emotionally unstable, and often agitated. At times he was pretty adventurous.

From the age of 25, he started experiencing depressive periods, with tachycardia attacks. He was terrified of death and hell, which triggered his depressive periods, especially in 1743, 1750, 1753, and 1756.

He moved to Charlotte, outside Paris, to spend more time in nature, but this did not improve his health significantly. He fell into religious and febrile moods more and more often. He tended to be a hypochondriac, and listed his symptoms, therapies, and doctors—doctors who eagerly treated him.

His psychological condition worsened to growing psychosis, with bouts of crying, deep melancholia, and with ideas of suicide.

Roland (Orlande) de Lassus (c1532-1594)

Orlando was a Flemish Renaissance conductor and composer. He had a stroke, which resulted in speech disturbance. In 1586 his mental and physical health worsened, so Rolande withdrew to the countryside, which helped him immensely. In approximately 1590, he became increasingly depressed, paranoid, and amnesiac, culminating in dementia.

Anton Bruckner (1824-1896)

Bruckner was an Austrian composer and organist. In St. Florian monastery, near Linz, he was a lonely boy who was taught music by music-teacher monks, the only people he could lean on sentimentally and sensitively. Being a profoundly neurotic person, only there was he accepted with understanding. He wrote: "I am always sitting, poor, lost and melancholic, in my little room." This melancholy was characteristic of many of his ancestors, his three sisters, and a mentally-retarded brother. He felt very lonely. When he was 21, he returned to the well-known St. Florian monastery near Linz to instruct the young men in musical knowledge and abilities.

Pyotr (Peter) Ilyich Tchaikovsky (1840-1893)

Tchaikovsky, "the porcelain child" or "the most romantic Russian composer," was a conductor, writer, critic, and educator. Fear of thunderstorms was a constant companion for him (and it is a theme he exploited in some of his works). His cigar addiction made him anxious and overly sensitive, and Pyotr struggled with low self-esteem, guilt, and a profound fear of death. He was pleasant, and interacted politely with others, but he was nervous and shy. Others, though, saw him as courteous and friendly. He experienced several nervous breakdowns, along with the accompanying night terrors and irrational fears. His demeanor was neurotic, and he had an effeminate air to his appearance. Unfortunately, he was neurotic and prone to making inappropriate adjustments.

His issues with women probably have their origins in his youth. His mother and governess, whom he had to say goodbye to at a young age, profoundly impacted his life, and he never overcame this.

Tchaikovsky wrote about his mother's passing: "Exactly five years ago my mother died. It was the first time I had experienced real grief and pain... Her death had an enormous impact on my own fate and the fate of my family. Every minute of that terrible day is still vivid in my memory as if it all happened only yesterday."

His German governess Fanny Dürnberg came in second place. She used to refer to him as her "porcelain child" because of his extreme sensitivity. Peter was just eight when she abandoned the family because of financial difficulties. Tchaikovsky grieved for days, and isolated himself from the rest of his family after hers departure.

Conclusion

This study included a survey of the ailments composers have experienced over the past five hundred years. The information gathered came from over ten thousand composers' biographies and more than a thousand other biographies. Composers' lives, as indicated before, were negatively impacted by the diseases and their comorbidities, which reduced their average lifetime from slightly more than sixty years to about fifty years. In addition, it had a destructive effect on their creative ability.

So now that we've heard how they struggled, let's see how they coped through what they composed—what magnificent compositions they created despite their most profound vulnerability. Can we consider the paragraphs below?

Tchaikovsky's earliest surviving work was written when he was fourteen. His mother's death inspired him to write his first complete composition, a waltz, *My Dear Little Mother*, which Tchaikovsky renamed *Mama*, incorporating it into Op. 39, *Album pour les Enfants* (1878).

Beethoven, instead of ending his life, as he had contemplated, returned to his art. On the advice of a friend, he picked up Shakespeare's *The Tempest* and subsequently composed the *Tempest* sonata. 1802 was one of his most productive years. The break in working may not have helped his health, but it allowed him to put pen to paper, and he contributed to the sonata and to variations for piano, composing the *Bagatelles*, Op. 33, and the *Variations*, Opp. 34 and 35. Symphony No. 2, Op. 36, marked a turning-point in Beethoven's career as a composer, as it was the first symphony he wrote after realizing that his hearing loss was permanent. His three piano sonatas, Op. 31, are also known as the *Tempest, Moonlight*, and *Storm* sonatas.

What about *Mozart* when, at 22, he had lost his status as a child prodigy? His mother fell ill and died while they were in Paris; and soon after, he composed the Piano Sonata No. 8 in A Minor, K. 310/300d. In addition, his Piano Sonata No. 14 in C minor (K. 457) was written in the summer of 1778, around the time of his mother's death--one of the most tragic times in his life.

The sonata is known for its emotional ferocity, and has been described as a reflection of Mozart's grief at the time. It is also regarded as one of his most essential works in his development of the classical piano sonata. Despite his difficulties, Mozart's piano sonatas demonstrate his mastery of the sonata form, as well as his inventive use of chromaticism, and his expressive harmonies that open the artist's soul like a book. Piano Sonata No. 14's emotional depth and technical complexity have kept it in the classical piano repertoire to this day.

Even though the young *Claude Debussy* was described by his classmates as clumsy, awkward, and highly unsociable, his music career began with his father's imprisonment during the war, and continued later--even though Tchaikovsky rejected some of his early work. Despite the initial rejection, Debussy went on to become one of the most influential composers of the late 19th and early 20th centuries, known for his innovative use of harmony and musical form. His works such as *Clair de Lune and La Mer* continue to be popular today. It's worth mentioning that he often wrote that even dressing himself was painful because of his cancer. He managed to write his famous (and only) violin sonata, premiered one year before he died. It was performed on September 14, 1917.

The young *Robert Schumann* injured his hand, and the resulting problems with his fingers ended

Schumann's piano career. The significant weakness of the middle and index fingers of his right hand gave him time to write amazing chamber music, and he laid the groundwork for the Romantics. Schumann's chamber music is known for its emotional depth and unique use of harmony, and it had an impact on the music of Brahms and Mahler. Despite his physical limitations as a performer, Schumann's contributions to classical music are still acknowledged today.

Let us look at the story of *Bela Bartok*. He missed several months of his second year at the Liszt Academy owing to illness, and later complained of pain in his right shoulder, and difficulty with playing the piano. From April to the middle of May 1940, he organized a concert tour in the United States. The tour included a prestigious appearance at the Library of Congress, as well as a recording of *Contrast* (1938), with violinist Joseph Szigeti, famous clarinetist Benny Goodman (who commissioned the work), and Bartók on the piano. Bartók's concert tour in the United States was a huge success, helping to establish him as one of the 20th century's greatest composers. His collaboration with renowned musicians such as Szigeti and Goodman (who recorded his work) aided in bringing his music to a wider audience.

Edvard Grieg left a lasting legacy, even though his work was described as 'old-fashioned' at the time. Grieg performed a concert of his own music in 1866, including some piano miniatures, and his first Violin Sonata. 1866 was the year of Nordraak's premature death. Nordraak was the Norwegian composer who wrote the country's national anthem, and his death was a significant loss to the Norwegian music community. Grieg was deeply affected by it. Despite his personal struggles, Grieg continued to compose and produce some of his most famous works during this time. During the summer of 1868, a year after his daughter Alexandra was born, and then died of meningitis, Grieg wrote his piano concerto in A-minor while on holiday in Denmark.

Anton Bruckner's Symphony No. 7 in E major is one of his most popular and frequently performed works. It is renowned for its majesty and emotional depth. The symphony exemplifies Bruckner's distinct style of combining traditional orchestral music with unexpected elements such as bird-calls and folk-melodies. It is regarded as one of his most personal and emotional works. People frequently praise the symphony for its use of Wagnerian harmonies, and its ability to transport listeners to a higher spiritual level. This piece was written between January and April, 1883, while Bruckner was affected by Wagner's death in the January of that year. Bruckner composed it after he'd returned to his roots in rural Austria.

Despite his creative psychosomatic brain disorder, *Rossini*'s creativity and talent were not affected, and he composed successful operas that are still widely performed today. His works showcase his ability to create captivating melodies and complex harmonies that have stood the test of time, such as *The Barber of Seville, William Tell,* and *La Cerentola.* Rossini's compositions are considered some of the most influential in developing Italian operas, the only operas that remain popular in modern times and are frequently performed in major opera houses.

Rousseau was a brilliant genius, philosopher, and gifted composer, His mother died while giving birth to him, and his father handed him over as a small child into the care of an uncle. He managed to establish himself and earn a living despite the difficulties in his childhood. He influenced the development of modern and educational thought. Rousseau became an early advocate of developmentally appropriate education; his description of the stages of child development mirrors his conception of the evolution of culture. In His book *Emile* he outlined his ideas on education, emphasizing the importance of individualized learning and hands-on experiences rather than rote memorization and strict discipline. Rousseau's theories continue to influence educational practice today. He composed *Le Devin du Vil-*

lage (*The Village Soothsayer*), which was performed for King Louis XV in 1752.

Many contemporary artists use their life experiences as inspiration for profound and moving works of art, proving that the concept of using emotions as a tool for artistic expression is truly effective. One of the Renaissance's most expressive and emotional works is Orlande de Lassus' *Lagrime*, a six-voice madrigal composed in the late 16th century. It is well known for its use of dissonance and chromaticism to convey the words' melancholy. Many believe that de Lassus' melancholy influenced the intensity of feeling and the complexity of thought in his music. Even though this piece was written in the late 16th century, even in this present century the creative brain is still not dignified, but is somewhat taboo. However, in the 21st century we can see how one's emotions and emotional blocks can be used poetically, as an expressive arts tool. This exemplifies how deeply emotions influence and motivate all forms of creative expression.

(look at the composers and their mental health challenges) Go to the research.

Working on my research, I found an old interview with Nicola Tesla, where he said " That the universe is alive in all its manifestations like a thinking animal. That the stone is a thinking and sensitive being, such as plants, beasts, and man. That a star that shines asks to be seen and if we were not self-absorbed we would have understood its language and its message."

He believed that the breath, the eyes, and the ears of man have to fulfil the breath, the eyes, and the ears of the universe.

He also talked about cosmic pain: where every time his close and beloved people were injured, he himself felt the physical pain. He explained to the journalist that this happens because our bodies are made from similar material, and that the soul is related to unbreakable filaments. That an incomprehensible sadness overwhelms us sometimes means that somewhere, on the other side of the planet, a child or generous man has died.

My thoughts are: Maybe at that moment that someone else experiences pain, these composers get the urge to write, and create masterpieces that can in the future be developed and researched even more deeply, to help with emotional and brain healing? Maybe depression can be healed in the composition? I know it might sound unreal and impossible, but what if we take (let's say) Brahms's *Hungarian Dance 1*, and compare that with the brain creativity of the composer, and find out whether he was composing that to heal others; because he might have felt sad or overwhelmed, and decided to compose the piece?

Musical notes can be healing. I believe that when matching the composers brain condition with someone else's brain that needs to hear those notes, it can be a tremendous development for the future. The composer's brain–now their music—can be linked to the creative health of the person who is experiencing sadness, trauma, or depression, or is blocked, helping to unblock himself and feel good again.

An example: We have a student who has the same creative health style as a Mozart had. What if we gave the student Brahms' *Hungarian Dances* to listen to: would it help him at the times when he is experiencing a sad or excited episode of brain creativity?

We can also try to examine the compositions, or music notes and harmony: use the QR code below to listen to the examination of the music notes and harmony. Apply, and research the theory I recorded for the different brain types.

Why would we even want to look at the scans of people's brains? What we would have to scan is the composition, and research the way we could further compose for the creative brain.

I'm coming to the conclusion that the imperfection in the composition could become perfection for someone: for someone the composition could be perfection, to create balance in the brain.

Let's just go back and look at Fibonacci and the golden ratio in music. He wanted to break the structure.

Forging a musical genre defined by Fibonacci sequences and the golden ratio necessitates throwing out long-held musical norms, and starting over with the fundamentals. In this mode, the arithmetical qualities of sequences like the golden ratio and Fibonacci numbers were transformed into melodic ones.

Although many past composers used these mathematical objects in their compositions, none made it the basis of their musical style. They needed to be ready to break the rules; or they were not allowed, as there was a specific style to compose in, based on the music-school technique and structure used. Probably they were trained to use the traditional structure, like ABA—a composing form, consisting of an opening section (A), a contrasting middle section (B), and a return to the material of the opening section (A).

Music and Different Abilities

Mozart began exhibiting his exceptional musical talent at the age of four. Although autism spectrum disorder was not a known concept then, his many unusual social behaviors included his sensitivity to loud sounds, his repeated facial expressions, and his repetitive body motions. His musical compositions also showed his inclination for repetition. Mozart was not an exception, as other composers wrote musical phrases with repetition, including Ravel (*Bolero*), and Orff (*Carmina Burana*).

These musical compositions connect, based on how the composers' brains were wired while socializing. I assume that many musicians who are differently gifted would be more receptive to such repetitive pieces, and would excel in performing and memorizing these without difficulty. This would open the door for differently-gifted children to perform in an orchestra, and might alleviate their feelings of isolation and loneliness—which was the case of Schumann, who was never diagnosed as suffering from any disorder.

Different arrangements and differentiated techniques could make the performance of these pieces by children with different abilities possible, having them perform as soloists accompanied by orchestras. There could be a division of solo chords between the soloist and the orchestra, based on the difficulty level.

Through my painting and composing techniques, and associating each string with a different color and then adding the notes and fingers that follows in the same color of the instrument string while adapting the composition for the violin or other string instrument I have discovered (and would like to explore further) that through these repetitions that the composers made, if we use color, we can see how their brain worked, and how maybe these colored patterns could contribute to starting to compose in that way—that it might reveal the right notes to boost performance, assist patience and focus, and contribute happier feelings and more positive thoughts for our creative brain style.

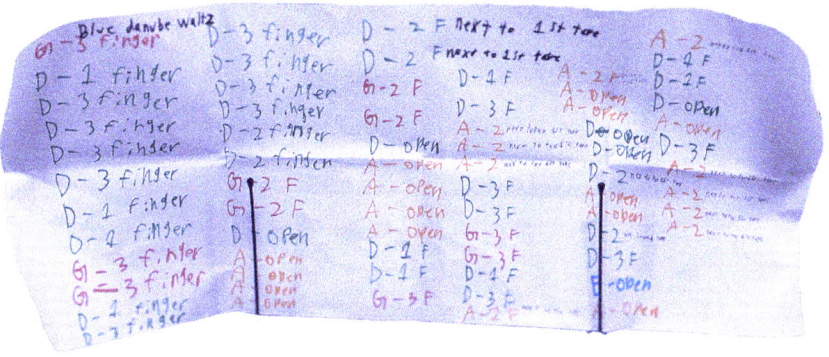

Another issue of great importance is knowing which musical composition to choose for our students. I always say 'Mozart' to kids, and 'Beethoven' to grownups. Why? Because of the musical style that Mozart carried from his childhood. We can't give Beethoven to a kid who still hasn't experienced the maturity and life of Beethoven; but we can provide Mozart, with fluffy and light music, like clouds, for the little hands, and happy notes for the ears. However, he was never satisfied, and could never compose something that would fill that emptiness when growing up as a kid, nor the mature experience he had in his adult years. We can use his music and his temperament for the small kids.

Beethoven was very emotional, stubborn, and introverted, though he looked like an extrovert. He composed Romances. We can't give a Beethoven Romance in F Major to a kid. He doesn't yet know what romance is. He needs to grow, to be a kid, and not copy the professors. And this is the mistake: setting the wrong piece that can be difficult to learn.

We can also provide some Bach music if the students are more philosophical, talkative, and curious. Bach had a lot of faith, and wanted to make everyone happy. He would sit at the piano and play every night to his wife and all his children, and they would sit next to him, and at the piano, and listen.

Additional music that is great for making young students eager to learn, for background and to encourage creativity.

1. Johann Strauss Tritsch-Tratsch-Polka Op. 214
2. Mozart "Eine Kleine Nacht Music"
3. Johann Strauss Radetzky March Op.228
4. Tchaikovsky The Nutcracker Suite op.79a
5. Camille Saint-Saens Carnival of the Animals
6. Shostakovich Suite for Jazz Orchestra no.2

If working with students both in the mainstream and with different abilities, this chapter will examine how we can use music to diagnose divergency. We will learn to apply techniques that we can always modify, and add new ones if we think this is required. We will also learn how to use the music instrument to diagnose possible differently-gifted children, and other brain creativity.

The purpose of the vignettes below is to demonstrate customized and differentiated music-teaching techniques to accommodate each student's unique needs. It is worth noting that several cases included in these vignettes are real-life cases, and all names were changed to protect the students' identity; however, there are a few fictitious cases that were included for the sake of demonstrating even more techniques that teachers would need when working with students with diffrent abilities.

Vignettes

Elena

Elena has recently started piano lessons after school. She is excited to learn some of her favourite songs but struggles with visual spatial reasoning and has a hard time keeping track of note location on the instrument. After speaking with Elena's mother, her music teacher placed colored stickers, each color on the corresponding note within each octave. The use of a stimulus prompt was especially helpful in improving Elena's accuracy with playing notes.

Student Age: 11

Teacher's Name: Sofija Zlatanova, Play Freely Music School

Domain(s) Addressed: Spatial Reasoning, Memory

Objective(s): Student will play a designated note on the piano using colored letter-stickers to identify the corresponding keys.

Materials:

- Keyboard (piano or practice instrument)
- Color stickers (3 sets of 7 different colors)
- Song book

Jordan

Jordan took piano lessons with the goal of being able to play his favorite song, "London Bridge". Jordan struggled especially with high attention deficit disorder, which always led him to ignore the correct fingering on the music notes; and as a consequence he was repeatedly playing the melodies incorrectly. This has been addressed by asking the student to slowly sing the numbers instead of the letter notes. Also, because of his hyperactivity he played incorrectly, very fast, and oftentimes began playing melodies from other songs. His teacher dealt with this issue by having him practice with a metronome, which gave him parameters of tempos to work within (e.g. go no faster than 52). He also considered it a game, trying to play at different tempos. Another issue he had to overcome during the lesson was the use of his left hand as well as his right. His teacher requested him first to play only using the right hand while she played the left-hand notes, and then the reverse, and then alternating roles. This gave him the ability to practice both hands separately and make a distinction between the use of each hand.

Student Age: 14

Teacher's Name: Sofija Zlatanova, Play Freely Music School

Domain(s) Addressed: Attention-deficit, hyperactivity, and boredom

Objective(s): Student will play a designated note on the piano using the correct fingering, and hand, and at the correct tempo

Materials:

- Keyboard (piano)
- Metronome
- Song book

Viktor

Viktor is a middle-school choir student and composer who has recently begun preparing for an audition. Part of his audition will consist of displaying accurate musical dictation, or writing down which notes and rhythms he hears when they are played. Viktor has fine-motor deficits and struggles to hold a writing utensil, so the audition coordinators have agreed to provide him with an iPad, or similar adaptive technology device, that will allow him to transcribe using only a touchscreen. The use of this type of application will ensure equality among all the participants in the audition.

Student Age: 12

Teacher's Name: Sofija Zlatanova, Play Freely Music School

Domain(s) Addressed: Fine-motor skills, Auditory Processing, Working Memory

Objective(s): Student will use an adaptive technology device to complete an audition involving musical dictation via a touchscreen and notation app.

Materials:

- Pre-recorded dictation melodies and rhythms
- iPad or similar device
- Notation app

Eduardo

Eduardo was learning to play scale C Major on violin. He was mainly struggling with lack of focus: he was extremely distracted, especially at the beginning of the lesson. Also, he had difficulty following instructions: for instance when his teacher was explaining what he needed to do, he simply kept playing. His teacher managed to remind him at the beginning of the lesson of the need to focus by offering him rewards, including taking a break to get his favourite food or perform an activity, before resuming the lesson. We found out that excessive praise worked exceptionally well for him. He also wanted to play faster and faster, which was addressed by using a metronome so that he could play at the right tempo. He had great ability to memorize songs and notes when he was focused.

Student Age: 9

Teacher Name: Sofija Zlatanova, Play Freely Music School

Domain(s) Addressed: Attention-deficit, ADHD

Objective(s): Student will play scale C Major on violin, two octaves on one bow

Materials:

- Violin bowings for scale (*legato*)
- Visuals to indicate that he should stop playing
- Metronome

Gordon

Gordon was learning to play scale C Major on violin, and specifically two basic dynamic indications: 'p' or piano, meaning "quiet", and 'f 'or forte, meaning "loud" or "strong". However since he lacked the needed attention and discipline to perform notes by sight-reading, he avoided reading notes at all, and therefore couldn't detect these dynamics. The process his teacher followed was first to work with him to apply adequate pressure on the correct fingers; to play quietly and loudly on one bow; and then do it up the scale. After enough practice to gain confidence, Gordon practised playing Vivaldi's *Spring*: then his teacher asked him to add in dynamics, and to alternate loud and quiet, by making gestures to indicate the change in dynamics. He did well, and had to practise more to make the quiet notes even quieter; but he was able to read the notes instead of typically using his great ability to play by ear.

Student Age: 12

Teacher Name: Sofija Zlatanova, Play Freely Music School

Domain(s) Addressed: Attention-deficit, aggressive communication tone, easily frustrated when challenged

Objective(s): Student will learn to detect dynamics on scale (*forte, piano*) or as described to Gordon: "Loud and Soft/Quiet"

Materials:

- Violin bowings for scale (*legato*)
- Visuals to indicate loud versus quiet
- Vivaldi: *Spring*

Martin

Martin is a high-school student diagnosed with ASD. He is an accomplished musician and is active in his school band, playing the viola. However Martin struggles with performance days, as they are different from his usual routine of school, practice, and homework. The change in schedule often causes him strong anxiety, which in turn frequently results in his forgetting important materials, such as his sheet music, or being late to performances. The school psychologist and his music teacher sat down with Martin to develop a visual self-monitoring checklist that covers essential actions Martin will need to do every concert day—such as washing and drying his uniform, double checking that his sheet music is in his backpack, and setting an alarm to leave for the performance—to increase his preparedness.

Student Age: 15

Teacher Name: Sofija Zlatanova, Play Freely Music School

Domain(s) Addressed: Memory, Self-Management, Executive Function

Objective(s): Student will increase performance preparedness by using a self-monitoring checklist.

Materials:

- Visual self-monitoring checklist
- Sheet music
- Uniform
- Instrument
- Anything additional needed for the performance, e.g., bottled water

Milan

Milan, who has sensory processing disorder, struggles with the feeling of touching a bow during his orchestra elective; however he has expressed an interest in learning to play the violin. Not wanting him to miss out on an opportunity to discover a new passion or skill, his music teacher provides him with a special sensory glove that Milan can wear on his bow hand. This glove, which is made from a material that Milan tolerates very well, provides him with necessary sensory input while still allowing him the dexterity needed to practice violin.

Student Age: 13

Teacher Name: Sofija Zlatanova, Play Freely Music School

Domain(s) Addressed: Sensory Processing & Integration, Fine-Motor Skills

Objective(s): Student will practice the violin using a sensory glove made from a well-tolerated material on the bow hand as needed.

Materials:

- Bow
- Violin
- Sensory glove

Rose

Rose was learning to play scale C Major on violin. She was mainly struggling with social anxiety disorder, and was fearful of being judged each time she played incorrectly or didn't understand the instructions. This led her to lose self-confidence ,as well as getting discouraged during the lesson, when learning something she is uncomfortable with. In order to make her feel more at ease, her teacher had her practice with half of the bow hair in front of a mirror to ensure that she only used the elbow, and that the wrist is always in the same position as the bridge, despite the feeling of discomfort that she might go through. This helped her tremendously, building her confidence, especially when she was practicing alone.

Student Age: 30's

Teacher Name: Sofija Zlatanova, Play Freely Music School

Domain(s) Addressed: Social Anxiety, fear of judgement, and low perseverance

Objective(s): Student will play scale C Major on violin, using only the elbow, while ensuring that the wrist is always in the same position as the bridge.

Materials:

- Violin
- Mirror
- C Major scale

Joe

Joe has recently started working with his teacher on his study skills to improve his grades in class. Joe is a bright student, but experiences difficulty with retention and recall of information. His teacher, familiar with making modifications for his students with ASD, noticed that Joe is very musically inclined, and can sing and play many songs from memory. He also frequently comes up with his own songs, and sings them in class. Joe's special education teacher spoke to the music teacher on campus, who has allowed Joe extra time in school each day to use the piano and guitar in the music room, to come up with fun, original melodies to which Joe can set important lines of text, or math equations. Joe also occasionally reuses the melody of a familiar song, but rewrites the lyrics to help him remember important notes from class. Using Joe's natural interest in music and composition to let him create his own study strategies has improved his test scores significantly.

Student Age: 13

Teacher Name: Sofija Zlatanova, Play Freely Music School

Domain(s) Addressed: Long-term memory, Multisensory Learning, Knowledge Recall

Objective(s): Student will use music to facilitate study skills and improve retention of academic content.

Materials:

- Notebook
- Instruments (piano, guitar)
- Notecards/flashcards

Can We Assess the Creative Health Brain by Playing and Studying, using an Instrument?

Abstract

This study investigates the effect of violin music lessons using creative and adapted teaching methods and materials with both mainstream and differently-gifted students. We will study and measure their focus, attention, behaviors, and learning speed. For this purpose, I will use the same creative teaching methods with students, and the same level of violin repertoire and technique.

Both students are beginners, and are from different backgrounds and cultures, but are they the same in their home practice, concentration, and responsiveness to detail?

The philosophical issues of diagnosis, and the underlying conditions affecting their final results, will be examined and compared, following brief definitions of the above-mentioned creative methods, and each student's learning stage.

Finally, the advantages and problems of using the same creative methods, and the responsiveness of the students with ASD, and the mainstream student, are explored for future education research and assessment into the student's implications, limitations, and opportunities for further study.

I will open with the question:

Do music material and teaching methods need more research and thinking outside the box for human brains?

"I am part of a light, and it is the music. The Light fills my six senses: I see, hear, feel, smell, touch, and think. Thinking of it means my sixth sense. Particles of Light are written notes. A bolt of lightning can be an entire sonata. A thousand balls of lightning is a concert... For this concert, I have created a Ball Lightning, which can be heard on the icy peaks of the Himalayas."

Figure 13

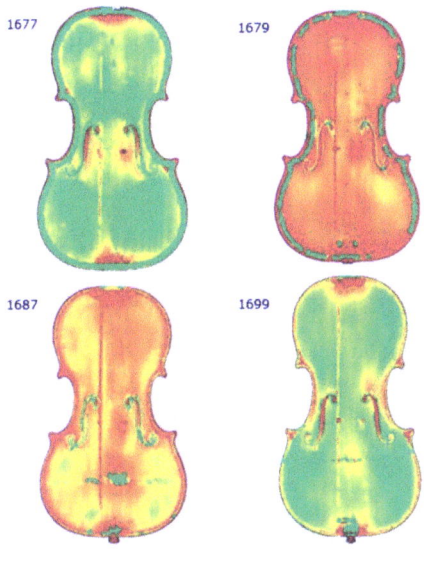

Hendry (2010)

Stradivarius Keywords: violin, music, special education, ASD, teaching, methodology.

As Nicola Tesla wrote, "Light fills his six senses, and he can hear, feel, smell, touch, and think".

I believe that with the power of music and positivity, bright, light music with spring water sounds, and the correct dose of creative teaching, tailored assessment for each student can be a transformation, and their instrument can serve as a tool to unblock, smooth, and assist every student, no matter their age or profession, when he or she is fighting with freeing the blockage inside the mind—which is one of the challenges that students with different abilities have.

Sometimes is difficult to push ourselves, but just as Einstein once said:

"Life is like riding a bicycle. To keep our balance, we must keep moving." But with the right amount of patience, and a suitable repertoire, one can feel empowered, which is our goal to achieve as educators for our students.

Music and those who are differently-gifted

Music has played a prominent role in the clinical and research literature on autism spectrum disorder (ASD) regarding diagnosis, therapy, and behavioral observations of exceptional artistic abilities, and has traditionally focused on social interaction, communication skills, and social-emotional behaviors. However, recently there has been an increased research focus on the role of motor and attention functions as part of the hallmark features of ASD (impaired social interaction), which may have significant implications for the role of music as an intervention for individuals with those who are differently-gifted.

Approaches to learning involve not *what* children learn but *how* they learn–their learning styles, attitudes, habits, imaginative capacity, motivation to learn, and openness to new tasks and challenges.

Knowing that, we will look at the profiles of the two students I chose, observe them through vignettes, and assess their musical focus, talent, and concentration. There will be two observations each for students A and B, one monitored and evaluated at the beginning of their work with me, and then the most recent.

Student A: **Male**

Age: 20

Nationality: Italian/American

Instrument: Violin

Years instrument Played: 3

Student-specific diagnosis: ASD

Student A, Vignette 1: *At the beginning*

My student A set up his violin and tuned it, I put the metronome on, and I did some warm-ups with him—whole/half/quarter/eighth notes. I also wanted to work with him on memorizing the pieces to help with his fluency in playing. I had him begin the piece Gavotte by Bach: without looking at the sheet music we played together, and I counted when there was a rest. When he played a note that did not match mine, he automatically restarted and corrected it.

He sometimes needs a couple of reminders of which note to play. Towards the middle, I told him, "Continue, B part." He struggled a little. Then I had him listen to the part as I played it. When he worked, he looked at my hand position as a cue. I prompted him through some of the notes when he needed this. I had him play it again to make it smoother. For the next part, I reminded him of the first two notes.

For a couple of the measures, I could see him correcting a repeated phrase that initially started with a b natural, then again with a b flat. I prompted him to use an up-bow several times, and he did it! I worked through to the end, which had repeated eighth notes that I counted off. Ultimately, I said, "Yay, you nailed it!" and we tapped bows together. We played that whole part again, and it was a lot smoother.

Then I had him work on another part in the middle of the piece, right before the b natural and b flat part. I was slowly working backward from the music, adding a few NOTES? before the initial measures he started with. I had him play by himself. This was an excellent glimpse into his ability to play fluently, considering that he memorized the ending part.

Conclusion

The memorizing by this student is so interesting to me. Usually, with students with different abilities, we frown upon that because we want them to learn how

to read the music. However, in his case, he knows how to read music, and uses this strength to understand the song initially. However, his music reading is later getting in the way of his fluency, because of whatever processing he needs to do in his brain. If he can memorize the piece, there will be less that he needs to do to progress.

A strategy based on Student A's individual needs as a learner: he needs to play from his memory and not worry about tracking the notes on the staff. I cannot wait to see how this method will help him progress over the weeks.

Student A, Vignette 2: *The latest progress*

We started working on scales. Student A needed help going between two high notes, so I had him practice going back and forth between the notes. He did that and then continued working on it.

Next, I had him play a piece (*Aura Lee*). I had him play through it, and he did a good job. I reminded him to play the ending twice.

After that, he chose to play *Canon in D*. I reminded him about the tempo change between the first and second parts, and told him to play the second part slightly slower. Then I modeled the tempo I wanted him to play. He then repeated it at that tempo.

Next, I had him play the Beethoven piece. He did an excellent job. Ultimately, I told him to play the music louder; otherwise, it was great.

After that, he played the *Blue Waltz* by Strauss. At the end I explained how to end correctly, and modeled it for him. Then I had him do it.

After that, I asked him to play the *Indian Story* concerto by Perlman. I reminded him that the first part was faster than the second part. He played it, and then I said that he did well but that I wanted more accent on the sixteenth notes. I played it to show him, and he repeated it. Then I told him he did great, transitioning between the two parts.

Next, I played a *Swan Lake* recording while he looked at the music. After that, he started playing. He had some trouble at first, so I told him to take his time and look at the music. After that, he did better. I told him that he has excellent intonation and should continue practicing that. I also told him that next time we would work on dynamics.

After that, he played the Brahms (*Hungarian Dance*) duet. I reminded him how it should sound and played a part for him. He played through, and I played when it was my part. He did an excellent job of waiting for me, to play his role. I then told him to make the end very short, and I played it for him, and he repeated it.

Next, I had him return to the refrain and played it for him. Then he played what I'd played, and continued. I reminded him that bar 34 has a C# and that the refrain needs to be slower. I played the right tempo, and he repeated it. I told him to remember to hold the bow for a few seconds in the end; and said that I would send him a recording of the Brahms.

After that, I told him we would work on *The Nutcracker*, a newer piece. He played it, and after, I told him, that he read it well. I told him not to go too fast, so he started playing it again, and I told him to stop at a part, but he kept playing. I do not think he heard me.

> I told him it was a good tempo when he'd finished playing, and explained how ballerinas danced to the music. I had him look at the music, and then I started playing, and he started playing and kept going. I told him to watch the ballet for this week's homework. Then I played a recording of *The Nutcracker* while he looked at the music. He then started playing the first page, and I told him that he did a good job, and to continue to work on it. He had to focus on Brahms, *Swan Lake*, and *The Nutcracker* for homework.

Conclusion

Listening to the recordings before playing helps the student with the tempo, intonation, and style, and is a very beneficial form of analyzing while listening. Looking at Vignette 1, when we had just started, and then my comments after some time, we have accomplished a level where he is comfortable playing medium-difficulty songs, unlike the traditional easy folk songs he was playing before we started working. Initially, we worked only on one piece at a time, and today we play a concerto, sonata, two or more music pieces, and scales at different tempos and bowing styles.

His parents reported that he is more motivated, encouraged, and focused, and feels great.

Student B: **Female**

Age: 33

Nationality: Slovenian

Years instrument played : 3

Student-specific diagnosis: Social Anxiety (no ASD)

Student B, Vignette 1: *At the beginning*

When I started working with Student B, she was at the level of playing straightforward beginner songs like *Twinkle, twinkle little Star*. The student was uncomfortable playing alone, but was used to playing with the teacher. She hoped she would perform better, and not make mistakes if she played solo. When introducing scales, she would quickly get discouraged after trying to repeat the incorrect note to make it correct. Moreover, when she found the right music note, it took much work to correct the pitch, as she thought she was achieving the right message.

No previous experience with scales; only one color of tape was placed on the violin's neck to better assist with notes (C Major 1 octave).

I started by working on the scale in one octave, and assigning different colors on each finger to the student as I created the C Major scale, with each note given a different color. Before that, I asked the student which colors she preferred, and she used her favorite colors. Gradually the student started learning the notes, and felt more comfortable reading the music. Then I introduced the *Aura Lee* song I'd arranged, with harmony as an accompaniment, but still gave the student the solo and leading part. I used this strategy to make the student feel comfortable, performing solo gradually.

Conclusion

Student B gets easily distracted after an unsuccessful tune. Furthermore, motivating her and getting her to accept that everything needs time to improve is hard. Technique, scale, and all of the learning process is a physical activity, the same as sport; and fingers need time, practice, and patience to learn the technique and piece, and to give our students strength while playing. The different colors my student chose worked for her. The base color scale that music educators use has the colors of the rainbow, but we should be more open and adapt to the colors that our student prefers to use, as they are better for their focus, concentration, and eye contact.

Student B, Vignette 2: *The latest progress*

When we started, I had her playing note by note. I would play it first, and then she would repeat it. Then had her play on her own. When she finished, I told her I wanted her to practice in front of a mirror so that the wrist was always in the same position as the bridge.

She told me it was uncomfortable, so I had her try playing with half of the bow hair.

I modeled it for her and had her try it. She said it annoyed her, but I told her it was because she was not used to it. I said she would practice using half of the bow hair for the first half, and the rest would be with the whole bow. She did it, but she still did not love it.

Then I told her to practice in front of the mirror and use half of the bow hair. I also explained to make sure she is only using the elbow.

Next, I had her play a piece, *Für Elise* by Beethoven. She had trouble remembering it, and I told her I would play one bar for her, and she would repeat it after me. I played the whole beginning of the piece to help her, then played the first bar and had her play it by ear. She had a little trouble with the D# and with C natural, so I helped her through it, and then she said she wanted to try it again, so I let her do that.

I could tell she was getting a little frustrated, so I told her to take her time and not to worry, and reminded her of the tape, and that the D# will always be on the third finger on the video.

She needed clarification about when something should be sharp or natural. For that, I explained the sharps and the naturals in the piece. I told her that if it would help, she could write an N under the naturals and an S under the sharps. After I explained all of that, she did much better.

Then I moved on to bar number 10, played it for her, and then had her play. She did well until she got to the C natural. For homework, I told her to write the N and S in the music, then explained that everything would be natural in this part. She played it again and suddenly realized why one sound was not right. She said she was putting down the wrong string, and went on to fix that.

After that, I talked to her about a high E and that I would not have her play that, but instead would have her play the second position E. Then I moved to the second page at measure 16, and she told me the notes. She did not realize that the sharp note carries through the whole bar, so I explained that to her, and she could play it. She had a little trouble, and I encouraged her again and said she was doing great. I also said that her son (8 years old, who plays piano) could accompany her because he knows the

> piece. I ended the lesson by encouraging her that she was doing great, and that this was a challenging piece.

Conclusion

From the beginning of our journey, student B progressed by playing, solo, moderate music pieces of the classical repertoire. Still, it took longer than student A on the ASD spectrum, unlike the non-diagnosed student B. I found that student B feels better and improves intonation with a tuner attached to the pegs of her violin while she is playing. In this case, the tuner would be assistive technology, unlike student A where we did not use any assistive technology. Student B progressed by learning one piece at a time, unlike student A who could play a few pieces at a time. Student A also had better focus and intonation immediately after recording, unlike student B who needed color-based tapes and a tuner.

All things considered

Comparing the two students and the advantages and problems of using the same creative methods, and their responsiveness in my research, resulted in the conclusion that the ASD student was able to do multitasks and more repertoire, and could be motivated very quickly; while the Mainstream student was easily discouraged, and anxious when trying something new to learn. The ASD student never complained. The Mainstream student used excuses like lack of free time to practice, and worries.

From my point of view, looking at the two students, I think that through more assessment, research, observation, and comparison, we can conclude that it is possible to diagnose those who are differently gifted and with other disorders. From my experience, I think that social anxiety and mental health should be researched and explored in students, because they might associate with ASD.

In the future, maybe physicians can use music and instruments to track the human brain instead of using scans like magnetic resonance, which is unsafe for human skin, and can lead to cancer.

If we can be more sustainable and care for the planet, why not care to be healthier in medical examinations? It is our body and brain, after all.

Music therapists, music educators, behavioral therapists, and scientists should always go one step further when thinking outside the box, and not rely on the old learning foundation, but build and improve on that and develop a new base, formed on different profiles, and strategies for each of those profiles, instead of using one assessment for all diagnoses and also for mainstream.

What Does It Mean to Be Critical?

On Inclusion, Diversity, Education, and Advocacy

From my Journals:

To be good professors, we must think up and create lessons and syllabi based on a theory and philosophy that will support the student's talent and further contribute to discoveries in music, science, and those who are differently gifted.

Alternatively, if we want to think outside the box, we can incorporate everything into a good curriculum and focused teaching, to help our students.

Universities and colleges have to follow the curriculum and syllabus, to be used in both public and private schools. However, we as educators cannot grow if we follow the same curriculum for every student. We have to look further into the future of education, rather than into the past. If we followed that path of looking back, how would we accommodate future minds still to be born, and educate them?

Through some of my Journals and crafted techniques, learning about inclusion, and the gifted students from my birth country, we can dive deeper into advocacy, inclusion, and critical thinking, which will help us create our techniques based on the student's goals and motivation.

The Journal posts are presented like a case study, to inspire the student's creativity and self-reflection. Use the QR code below to read more.

What have been our obstacles in the philosophy of American music education?

Why does the philosophy of good education sometimes fail?

- More involvement is required from parents.
- There is a need for more funding for music technology equipment in the classroom.
- There is the same old curriculum, with unmotivated educators...
- There are challenges to adapt to the student's needs, especially children with different abilities.
- The classrooms are overcrowded, with no assistants for inclusive Music Education.
- There is a lack of programs for the talented and gifted, and for diversity in Music Education.

All the above can qualify as obstacles, and play a significant role in limiting the education of young pupils, and of future generations.

What if we provide a learning environment that is engaging for students who need to learn better than they do in the traditional classroom model? We want to change many things as educators; but sometimes, as perfectionists (because of our artistic and instrument-performance backgrounds), we always think that we are not enough. And not only sometimes, but most of the time, we *are not* sufficient.

Most of the issues mentioned above can be because of political pressure, and lack of funding towards building a sound philosophy of Music Education without obstacles or challenges.

The Educator can't be creative, and make changes or adaptations to the curriculum, because it represents the particular public or private university, and must remain as it is. So the educators/professors can't modify the curriculum to suit the individual student in the classroom, so making it more inclusive. It is one curriculum for all--for everyone that most public and private schools offer.

How do we correctly place American Music Education history in a context?

It all started with the social singing societies.

With the help of the singing teacher Lowell Mason, Boston decided to include Music as a curriculum subject.

Pestalozzi's theories, on the other hand, bring high value to sensory, kinesthetic, and active learning.

Music Education, primarily vocal, remained most common in women's schools. However, many private academies also existed, offering boys and girls instruction in orchestral instruments like the violin, viola, cello, and piano.

The foundations of American Music Education were laid in the nineteen century.

Instrumental education was offered later, in private schools, and vocal singing/chorus was taught throughout the public schools.

Music: is it defined as just one stand-alone curriculum subject?

It has been shown that the study of music increases the brain's ability to process sound, and distinguish differences in sound.

Beyond the neurological benefits of using music to develop literacy, one can also use music to examine literary concepts in the classroom. Poetry is an excellent illustration of the connection between music and language.

Another great idea is that of using musical games to teach students to listen critically, and help develop their aural awareness. Games can be an excellent teaching tool for keeping students engaged; for example, using music flashcards with them, or giving them a task to draw music notes inspired by their favorite movie scene, or game.

Music can be good as a subject, and also help the students with other subjects, such as math, language, and other liberal arts classes.

"Teaching and finding freedom"

In the real world of pedagogy positions, as educators we must continually discover and rediscover openings ourselves.

Sometimes, what we see as universal, and suitable, can shock us because of the different viewpoints surrounding us; and these may pressure us to shift.

We need to question (twice!) our philosophy of thinking and ideas, and decide whether that place or position we are looking at is the right choice for us. Remember: the place where we choose to work should feel like Confucious once said: "Do what you love."

As diverse souls, it isn't easy to find the freedom and courage to mold ourselves as unique educators, and respect our students, when we live in a world where hierarchy still exists, and the student is never right.

These are only my thoughts and philosophy: to some, it might be Jazz (if you know harmony, you can understand this!).

So, if you are a good teacher and want to make changes, you can fight the system where you are now, with invisible and small steps; or start your own course, and deliver your ideas.

How Will You—the Teacher, and Your Class—Adapt to Virtual Spaces (Post-Covid)?

From my perspective as a violin teacher, we have first to educate the parents and students on how to prepare for a webcam violin or piano lesson.

As soon as the pandemic started, I prepared small handbooks for the parents about live online lessons, and how they differ from face-to-face lessons, as there are several moving parts. It is essential to be sure that their children/my students are prepared. So I gave them a few tips on testing before our lessons began.

I asked them to ensure that they had a strong Internet connection, and could log into their preferred communication platform, whether Skype, Google+, or something different that they or I had chosen. I like to use Skype because I have all of my students there, and I can quickly call them when I finish teaching another student. All the parents have to do is log in when it is time for the lesson. Suppose they have never used the platform, or not used it in quite some time? In that case, I tell them not to just hop on five minutes before their lesson begins, but to log into the platform 15-30 minutes before classes start, to make sure that everything is running smoothly, and to test the video and audio quality.

A common mistake when having a webcam violin lesson for the first time, I found with my students, is that they stand on the wrong side of the screen, or face the wrong way so that I cannot see their bowing! They must ensure that their music stand is on their left as they look at the computer screen, not on the right!

Being a good teacher equipped with Psychology of Education is essential. It is challenging, and only some people are used to the new normal, post-Covid. We may stay where we are now for quite a long time, and it can be an emotional challenge for our students, and for us. I always take five minutes from lessons to ask them how they are feeling, and what they have been doing.

What is Beauty? What is Beautiful in Art?

Beauty takes different forms and has different types. There is beauty in everything, but not everyone can see it. Moreover, there is an art of knowing how to appreciate beauty. Beauty in Arts, Beauty in Thoughts, Beauty in Music. Beauty in pictures captures a moment of perfection that remains. Beauty can be in the golden ratio, or the sequence of Fibonacci numbers.

We are the creators, and we should be open-minded enough to find beauty in the ugly, because we can learn from even the unlovely, which can serve as comparative literature to any horrible life experiences, and show us how we can improve our lives, and help others.

Inclusion in North Macedonia

To be inclusive educators, we must also be aware of what is happening around the globe, in both some undeveloped countries and some developed ones. Living with the stigma... How can we help transfer that knowledge, and advocate from where inclusion is respected to a country where it is not? I will talk about my country, and its Portraits of Children with Autism and Special Needs in Macedonia, and their families fighting for their right to inclusive education.

Imagine what it would be like if your life were reduced to what you can see. Could you see the feelings, the thoughts, the impressions? What would you do if you needed visual support to function in the outside world?

In Macedonia, the general public gained some knowledge about the symptoms of the disorder of being differently gifted with the screening of the film *Rain Man*, filmed in the late 1980s, in which Dustin Hoffman, with excellent acting, depicts the clinical signs of being differently gifted. In 1995, a seminar, "Autism and other child psychoses," was organized in Struga. The etiology, clinical picture, diagnostics, treatment, and the need for collective forms of treatment in the Republic of Macedonia were discussed.

On May 22, 2000, the Macedonian Scientific Association for Autism (MNZA) was founded, which includes special educators, psychiatrists, doctors, immunologists, allergists, epidemiologists, psychologists, and other professionals.

During the short period of its existence, MNZA started with several activities—registration; presentation to the Macedonian public through the media; membership of the European Associations, Autism Europe and EASPD; a presentation of the project information on Autism in Macedonia, where two pamphlets were produced, and two web pages were created. Members of the Ministry of the Interior also participated in two scientific research projects.

People who are differently gifted in the Republic of Macedonia were neglected until recently, and their problems were pushed to the margins of Macedonia's priorities. So far, no conditions and systems for solving their issues have been created (there are no appropriate institutions for treating these children, and the rights of these children have not been specified and formalized).

They were discriminated against in enrollment from kindergarten, rejected, and left at the mercy of the personal policies of principals, teachers, and schools. They were faced with totally unprofessional staff, and a massive shortage of professionals and special educators in all segments of their education. The parents of children with different abilities unanimously agree that this is an accurate picture of the exclusion of their children in Macedonian education.

Inclusion in education is a process of mutual respect for each student's diversity and needs, where the student is the center of attention. The education system needs to address the challenges facing all students. This implies that the schools' material, financial, and personnel resources have to be ready to respond to the needs of students in regular classes, providing curricula and aids that will be adapted to individual capacities and conditions, and suit their affinities. However, students with twice exceptional get something very different from Macedonian education.

Equal opportunities for everyone, with knowledge working against prejudice.

I want to help!

The difference is astonishing.

We are all friends.

What are the Parents Saying?

They are saying that according to the law, there is inclusion; but in practice, the experience is very different. They face discrimination daily, and the education provided for their children is not even close to equal. It needs to be more proactive.

"Our children are not subjects. We want actual involvement in education! "

"I transferred my child to a school for children with special needs after he failed to spend two years in a regular school. The teachers were not trained; some did not want to be, and some did not know how to deal with him. We were obliged to be in the school because we took him from one classroom to another when the classes were over, and there were transfers to the toilets; there was no special educator, and we did not have enough money to pay for an escort or professional help. The child did not progress. "Our children deserve real inclusion if they don't already have it," said Jasna, the mother of a child who is twice exceptional.

Our 'inclusion' is confusing. From the beginning, I encountered barriers, rejection, and stereotypes from the teacher and the children's parents.

"The teacher did not want to work. Honestly, she did not even know how to work with Monica. She told me that we are not trained to work with children with special needs," said Ivana, Monica's mother. Monica is in the eighth grade at a regular school, and is from Bitola.

Ivana says they transferred Monica to another school after two years of discrimination. "We were forced to change schools: my daughter, who has combined developmental disabilities, took a one-year break, so we enrolled her in another school in Bitola. At least there is a special educator here, the only one in the city."

"When you enroll your child in school, you see how they reject you, and do not accept you."

Elena, Ivana's mother, who is diagnosed with elements of the autistic spectrum, faces similar problems of discrimination. And educational staff are unprepared, and scared to work with children who are twice exceptional.

"According to the law, I could not be rejected; but you feel that energy, you know: you see when you are undesirable. Usually, in regular schools, they look to reject you, not to accept you. When you go to enroll your child, they do not say "Bring it, we will do our best", but they convince you that you cannot enroll it," says Elena.

She says there is no special educator in the school where her son from Prilep studies, and the special educator from the municipality never came to work.

Marija, the mother of a child who is twice exceptional from Bitola, says that she sends her son to school accompanied by a psychologist: there is no special educator in the regular school where he goes, and the school psychologist has never asked how he is, or what her child's diagnosis is.

"The school psychologist did not work with him once, nor did he say, "Good day; what is wrong with the child?" He does not know his diagnosis. "Our child is accompanied by a psychologist, whom we pay for ourselves; there are several children who are twice exceptional here," she said.

What is the Response of the Institutions and the Educators in Macedonia?

These children learn according to the regular curriculum, by making individual educational plans. The teacher prepares the project in cooperation with the pedagogue, psychologist, and parent, but there is no special educator! There is no tailored educational program.

Regarding assessment: according to the teachers, the evaluation is disputable because it is not defined anywhere, so these students are assessed by whoever they want to do this. The grading system in elementary/secondary schools in Macedonia is from 1, to 5 as the highest. If the child has achieved all the goals according to the program, he would score a five. However, some teachers compare the progress of diverse-needs children with the other children's achievements, giving them only a 3, the mid-point. So it all comes down to the goodwill and sensibilities of the teacher.

Students' academic success is positively correlated with the quality of their relationships with their teachers. Positive teacher-student relationships encourage learning, and make students want to know—as long as the course material is engaging, age-appropriate, and a good fit for the students' abilities.

Envision a situation in which a student and teacher have a positive working relationship, and the student receives more encouragement and guidance from the teacher than criticism.

As a result, they are more likely to respect their educator, take an active interest in her classes, behave responsibly, and succeed academically.

This demonstrates the significance of students' positive relationships with their teachers for their academic success. Teachers who put their students' needs first can significantly impact their academic and behavioral outcomes. They form strong bonds with their pupils.

The burning problem is the external assessment, because the students take tests based on the general primary curriculum, rather than an individual one.

There need to be more professionals in Macedonia, and the need for more special educators is one of the main problems in implementing inclusion.

In Bitola, specifically in only one school, a special educator is employed in "Kliment Ohridski." He works only in the home school. There is no special educator or speech therapist in Krushevo.

What do children and parents in small towns face? A significant percentage of children from these families are social cases, and do not have the financial means to pay for a companion or professional assistance.

What is the Ministry of Education saying?

The Ministry of Education and Science says that they are committed to strengthening the professional psychological-pedagogical service in schools. They say that the schools, teachers, and parents of students with special educational needs should make individual plans and programs for working with these students. Still, in a survey on including children who are twice exceptional in regular education responded to by 265 schools, it was concluded that only some schools are ready to provide adequate education for a child who is twice exceptional:

Center for Children with ASD in Tetovo, Macedonia

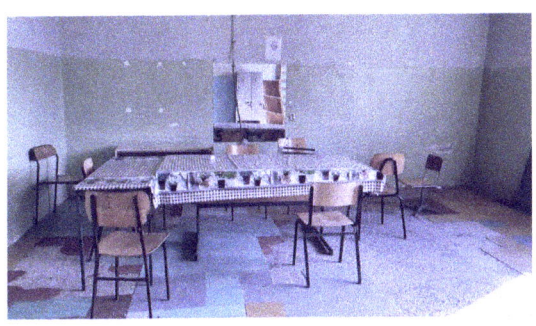

The Institute of Rehabilitation for Children with Special Needs is in Skopje, Macedonia

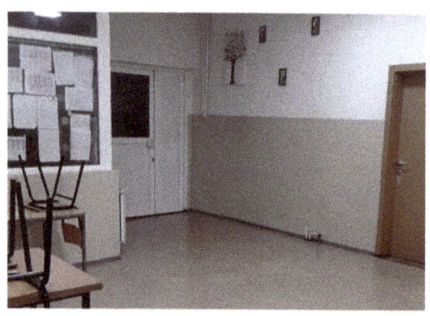 

Special Elementary School Zlatan Sremac, Skopje

AND IN ADDITION TO THE RIGHTS OF CHILDREN WITH AUTISM: Schools are not ready for their education — research by the Ombudsman.

(Title translated from the article)

Conclusion

Better legislation and training of teaching staff are urgently needed.

Discrimination in education against children with disabilities is unacceptable. Such discrimination is illegal because the primary and secondary education laws guarantee the right to adequate education for children who are twice exceptional. Additionally, discrimination is against international legal norms. The Republic of Macedonia is a member of all relevant international human rights conventions, especially the Convention on the Rights of Persons with Disabilities, and the Additional Protocol to it, which have committed to respecting, and providing all human rights and freedoms for persons with disabilities.

To improve the situation, the competent institutions, especially the Ministry of Education and Science, should take urgent measures, by improving the legislation regarding the education of children with disabilities and their proper inclusion in the education system. It is necessary to create appropriate teaching staff, in qualitative and quantitative terms, who will be employed in educational institutions in the country. As a first step, it is possible to organize appropriate training for part of the teaching staff, so as to have at least a small team capable of teaching children with disabilities in all primary and secondary schools.

Improving the infrastructure for access and smooth movement of children who are twice exceptional in school facilities is necessary.

Investment in Technology for students who are twice exceptional is essential.

Because this issue has yet to be paid much attention to by the competent authorities in the country, it is necessary to take urgent measures to provide at least the minimum standards as soon as possible, until gradually the problem is fully resolved.

Let us look at the world from a different perspective. It is time for professionals and the government to take the needs of people who are differently gifted seriously, and to try to make the world brighter, more attractive, and more accessible to them. Their success is the success of us all.

Crafting For and Working with the Gifted Multimedia Student

Differentiation as a Learning Objective (in my classes)

Differentiation as a learning objective refers to the ability of teachers to modify their teaching to meet the diverse needs of their students. This approach helps ensure that all students are challenged and supported in their learning, regardless of their background or ability level. Engaging all types of learners is beneficial because it promotes learning at their own pace. And for some students, that is of great importance because not everyone can learn at the same speed. It is like using presto, moderato, or prestissimo, when some students are used to lento or adagio.

I will teach them about Mozart's opera, *The Magic Flute*: Magic Flute

In each class we will explore a different aria from *The Magic Flute*.

For this class I've chosen the aria *Papageno* from *The Magic Flute* - part 1: from the beginning of the aria to 0:25.

The teacher will be Papageno—the male voice

The students will be Papagena—the female voice

During the instrumental music they will hold their hands on their ears.

These are the teaching steps, including the winding back and winding forward:

1. As the music starts with the instrumental introduction, we will hold our hands on our ears, waiting for the teacher to make her entrance with "pa pa pa pa."
2. Then when the female voice comes in, the students repeat "pa pa pa pa."
3. Then teacher again sings "pa pa pa pa pa pa pa pa."
4. Then the students sing "pa pa pa pa pa pa pa pa."
5. Then the teacher sings "pa pa pa pa pa" (in a different rhythm).
6. Then the students repeat this.
7. Then the teacher sings "pa pa pa pa pa Papageno."
8. Then the students sing "pa pa pa pa pa Papagena.
9. Then the aria ends: the first part.

Now the teacher will be Papagena, and the students will be Papageno.

Now, some different actions, instead of hands on their ears:

Hands on their arms

Hands on top of their heads

Using only one finger, or two, or three, or five

Singing "la la la" instead of "pa pa pa"

Singing "pa pa" only twice, and twice in their heads

Singing "pa pa" twice forte, and twice piano

Standing up when the male sings

Sitting down when the woman sings; and then the other way round

Students can choose to sing their own names instead of "Papageno" (the teacher can ask who would like to give us his or her name to sing here: for example "vi vi vi vi vi Vicky" instead of "pa pa pa Papagena", or "da da da da da David" instead of "Papageno". They can continue with this until they've used all their names.

It's just the right song!

Choosing a song in the music classroom that doesn't have a pitch, so that all students, musical or not, can succeed, is a good thing. This method creates a learning environment where all students can take part and feel good about what they are able to do. It also promotes the development of other musical skills, such as rhythm, dynamics, and expression.

When we have many students in the classroom, and we also have students who are not musically gifted or inclined, we have to pick an appropriate song to match the students' musical talent.

Selecting an appropriate song that doesn't have pitch means using a song that students will never sing with a perfectly focused tone, pure intonation, or a balanced texture.

In this case, I use dissonance.

I place stickers on the floor in different colors, representing the easiest chord: do, re, do.

I first start by jumping with my feet on the stickers. Another way to show this is to pass a ball to them in turn, and they each stand on the stickers. I can show them the pitch distance that way as well. Then I will ask the students about this.

I dance, and sing the dissonant chord, but not properly; and then ask them to do the same jumping, or dancing, and singing, or any combination of these.

After I've achieved this, I add one more tone to jump on, on the floor. With them dancing, the pitch will tremble, which is perfect for a no-tune song, and they will feel that they know the song.

Introducing the Violin: the First Lesson—How to Begin?

I always want to start with an explanation of what we will go over today in our lesson, and what we will learn. With some students, I make a schedule with checkmarks, and with some, I don't. I feel that they don't all need the structure of the lesson to check all the assignments and learnings in the lesson: they just like to go with the flow, and they feel that it doesn't impact their learning. I like to honor that. Not every lesson has to have a schedule and be organized, even when we work with children of different abilities.

So let's take a look.

The lesson starts:

Today we will learn about the right hand. The natural motions of the right arm, hand, and fingers in the technique of holding the bow. The bow is made of wood, and hair from a horse's tail, onto which we add rosin.

The rosin is applied to the bow hair to create friction against the strings of the instrument, which produces the sound. This is an essential step in playing stringed instruments such as the violin, viola, and cello.

Before we begin, I want you to:

- Imagine flexibility in your arm, hand, and fingers—as natural as you feel in your legs, feet, and toes when you walk.

- We will begin with holding a pencil, as that is the easiest way to feel how the fingers should be pointed on the bow. Just take the pencil from the table, in your hand.

- This is how it should feel: light, but strong enough to allow your fingers to hold it: not putting too much pressure on it, just enough to produce a sound or letter if we are writing on paper.

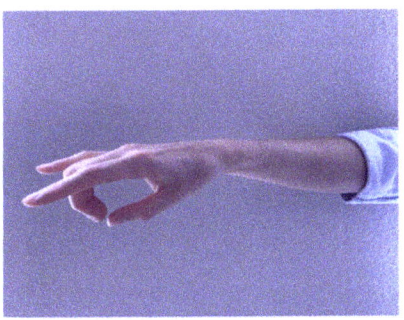 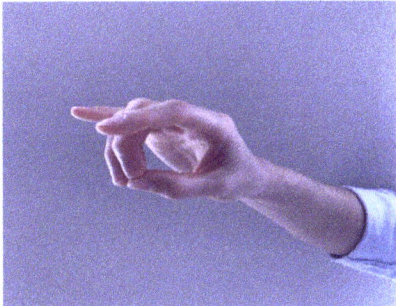

- Look at your fingers. The contact points of the thumb and the second finger are together now: let's add the middle finger and make a trio.

- Now I want you to take the bow and hold it as if it were the pencil.

- Now add the 4th and pinkie fingers. Bravo!
- Now before we place the bow on the strings, let's make the index finger the leader!
- Just slightly turn him towards the left side. Imagine that he is always tired!

Now he is ready to meet with the strings and create the sound that you wish!

Drawing as a Tool to Introduce Music Lessons to Beginners

Some of the children with autistic spectrum disorders are visual learners. When teaching, my cues and practice guidelines need visual reinforcements and prompts. If I find out that my student loves to draw, we draw the music that we will play that day, or will start to learn.

If I have to introduce the Strauss Waltz as a music piece, we will learn together by drawing while listening to the music piece. Then we name the composition, according to the colors that we were using. In one case, we used blue to paint the horse that my student got inspired by and drew while listening to the *Blue Danube Waltz*, and we called it the *Blue Horse Waltz*. Immediately the student connected with the piece and wanted to start learning. This also benefits the student's ear training, as listening repetitively helps the student to connect better.

I always love giving them plenty of colored pencils to choose from. It is essential to bring us closer as friends, and to break the barrier created between teacher and student by labeling them and giving them roles.

We have first to be their friend, and then their teacher.

Let him or her talk to the teacher about his or her day, friends, likes and dislikes, plans, etc. Talking about these things helps create a connection, after which music can be introduced.

Picture Books that Guide the Instrument in Melody Production

Music educators can use picture books as a multidisciplinary learning tool to connect with beginners when they are learning an instrument.

It is an excellent tool for improvisation when they are just starting to learn the notes. They do not have to know all of the letters to play.

Suppose I see that my student, when touching the piano for the first time, comes up with a melody of even one bar, yet is unaware of the music notes. In that case, I open one of my picture books on the stand, and read it to my student. When I stop at one section of the story, he starts to improvise, based on the story of the book section. I always give them a choice.

Two of the books that I use are *Pete the Cat's World Tour*, and *Over in the Meadow*. This way, my student feels he is the composer, and the accompanier, and is very proud of these two accomplishments.

Songs with simple repeated musical themes are used for faster learning, and an incredible feeling of accomplishment.

We must choose a repetitive classical piece when working with a special kid.

Twinkle Twinkle, Little Star, Beethoven's *Minuet*, or Pachelbel's *Canon* are magical when you want them to accomplish fast, feel great, and learn the sonata form of ABA[8] when introducing music theory.

I always make sure to have and to know the song's harmony to support my student in the learning process, and accompany him/her as a second instrument. It is important again to prioritize them as the soloist. I always say, "You are the leader, and I will follow you".

---

8 ABA — a composing form, consisting of an opening section (A), a contrasting middle section (B), and a return to the material of the opening section (A).

Learning a Scale on the Piano with Alphabet Symbols and Numbers

Depending on the creativity of the child, and his gift for letters or numbers, math or drawing, when we are introducing the C Major scale of do-re-mi-fa-sol-la-ti-do, or c-d-e-f-g-a-b, we can use stickers with alphabet letters, numbers, or pictures of an animal or fruit that starts with the first letter of the scale.

One example: C is for Cat, or Car, and we can ask the student to add the sticker with the car symbol or letter in the appropriate place for the C note on the piano.

The same works for numbers: C can be 1, and D can be 2. It all depends on the appropriate assessment of the student by his music teacher. What is the way he wants to learn to play, and what does he favour: letters, numbers, or pictures!

Follow the interests of the child who is differently gifted on the piano, and they will lead you to their success.

Devise movements to accompany listening experiences with Vivaldi, and teach the difference between an orchestra and a soloist.

When we want to teach our students about an ensemble or orchestra, or the range of different music instruments, and how they should listen to classical music (a symphony, or a quartet), we can play them a classical music piece like Vivaldi's *Four Seasons*, with a violin soloist, and engage them in musical problem-solving.

First, the teacher will be the soloist and the students the orchestra.

When the teacher starts to move, it means that the soloist is playing, and they will have to stay in one place; when the orchestra enters, the students will be moving/dancing in their own way, based on the song's rhythm.

Another way can be to interpret the instruments' sounds. For example, students move like birds to accompany bird-like sounds as they listen to Vivaldi's *Four Seasons*.

My Tips For Lesson-planning

As teachers of programs for those who are differently gifted, we always have to choose materials that are age-appropriate, developmentally accessible, and motivating.

When creating lessons, it is good to set both non-musical goals as well as musical ones. An example is improved social interaction and communication. When teaching, provide direct instruction in social skills as needed.

Many children who are differently gifted benefit from a structured learning environment. So: follow a routine to ease transitions, and use repetition and reinforcement to teach skills. Visual aids can help explain rules and procedures, list daily schedules, and illustrate songs. Offer students choices of what music to play, which instrument to choose, or which pencil color to use to write down the notes. If the child is non-verbal and uses an alternative communication system, like an iPad or flashcards, utilize the same system in your class, and see that music vocabulary is added.

When you understand your individual students' strengths, deficits, and sensory impairments, you can modify your plans so that everyone can succeed at something.

Sometimes we may have a student who cannot tolerate the sounds of specific rhythm instruments. Find an instrument he can play, or give him the choice of singing or dancing instead—or a combination of both. If a child cannot sing, or play a string instrument, allow him or her to choose a rhythm instrument.

Keep going even if an activity seems to fail initially; when you find something the child connects with, you will know it! Remember to network with your colleagues, as they may have some helpful ideas. The special education teacher and the therapists may have valuable insight to share, to help the students they work with daily.

Find out what strategies work in other settings, and adapt them to your needs. Adaptation is a *must*, and when creating the lesson plan we should always leave room for modifying a lesson strategy.

General Strategies

To improve communication and social skills, and encouraging and reinforcing positive social interaction, it may be wise to ignore some behaviors as long as they do not interfere with the lesson. If you plan to have children work in small groups, like for chamber music or a duo, with both mainstream students and those with unique gifts, carefully select which children will work together. More sensitive mainstream students can better assist and understand the child with extraordinary skills.

Be mindful of any sensory impairments in your students, and reduce sensory input where necessary. For example, decrease the amount of visual clutter in your room, or lower the volume of music that you play. Make the room where you teach more minimalistic, and simpler, but colorful for good and positive energy. Colors can sometimes boost our mood and mind, especially green. (Learn more in Chapter 2, in the section *The Theory of Nutrition*.)

Allow time away from class if sensory input is too intense: walking to the front door, or a trip to the library, or another classroom, can significantly help in this situation.

When behavioral problems arise, remember that these may result from difficulties with communication, social skills, and sensory issues, and are not acts of open resistance. After problems occur, analyze the behaviors, pinpoint what may have triggered them, and adapt your methods accordingly. A behavior management system based on positive reinforcement can be helpful. The teacher has to make the student feel safe in the classroom. Moreover, teaching peers how to interact with the student will be beneficial for all, and at the same time will foster a sense of empathy and kindness in other students.

I always ask my students to tell me what makes them feel safe.

How Can Music Help in Early childhood?

How can we tell if a child has what it takes to be a violinist? Is it possible? Yes. If we see that the child is quiet and speaks softly, and we see that he or she performs some dance movements to music that plays in the background, we can try and give them an instrument, especially the violin. If we see that they are able to hold their head in the violin's chin rest so that the violin is at the right angle, they can start as early as two years old, by first practicing with a violin made from soft material, and a soft bow. If we leave the room, and they start exploring the violin by themselves and practice in a corner, we know that the child is gifted, and has potential.

When children are young, music can help their brains grow, their language skills improve, and their memories get stronger. Additionally, music can also aid in emotional regulation and socialization.

Students on the spectrum may find music an especially fruitful area for development. Children can benefit from learning to work in groups and ensembles, to perform songs, dances, and instrumental music, because it encourages them to interact positively with others. A child's ability to speak, imitate others' voices, focus longer, and express themselves creatively can benefit from exposure to music.

What follows is a list of ways kids of various ages can benefit from listening to music.

Let's begin with the musical prodigies among the youngest members of our species.

To aid in a baby's cognitive growth, music is crucial.

A class showing them how to make music, or an introduction to different instruments, can be a great place for them to start finding their voice.

Unlike pre-schoolers, who are active walkers, and learn a great deal outdoors, musical imagination, zeal, and competence flourish for babies during time spent indoors. However, playing games outdoors and encouraging them to move to music can be a great outlet, and lead to faster learning.

The little leader grows in stature. When you have your violin or piano lesson, it's great to give the kids time to play their favorite game, watch a scene from their favorite movie, or play together during the break. Older kids like challenges, structure, and fun with rules. I enjoy a good game of bow fighting with a student. It'll assist him with his homework if he triumphs.

What are Some of my Objectives when Educating the Young Gifted Student?

Objectives are essential before we develop a lesson and year-plan for our students, for achievement in the instrument, or in general music. These are some goals I create and follow, and I often add, adapt, or change them if needed, depending on my student's needs.

I want my student to develop an inquiring mind, one with confidence, and music manners.

I want my student to learn to communicate effectively, in both verbal and written form, through music and notation.

I want my student to learn to acquire information from various sources, and record findings in multiple ways, including using digital technology in music.

I want him or her to understand comprehensive theory, and establish musicianship.

I want him or her to understand basic scientific ideas and concepts through composing.

To gain a basic understanding of historical and geographical skills and knowledge through music history.

To appreciate the joys and benefits of physical education, and experience a range of parent-student activities.

Furthermore, ultimately, I want them to use music, drama, and art/craft skills for creative expression.

I want them to learn how to spend their leisure time imaginatively, independently, and collaboratively; and I encourage them to practice at home.

As an educator and student myself, I always want to learn new ways and techniques, to have better objectives, and to explore better goals for my students' knowledge. We have to love our profession to teach young pupils.

Lesson Plan Ideas, Using Music Technology.

It is time to compose, so I chose a student to write a melody of 4 bars, in his chosen scale, in one octave.

We will build the composition weekly, with one row of the music staff (4 bars). After the student composes the 4 bars, he will draw the notes in a suitable *Soundtrap*.[9] After finishing these two assignments, he must write a libretto for the 4 bars. The lesson must be taught step by step, especially when my students are twice exceptional. I will be their partner in this activity.

We must be straightforward in our exercises and assignments. This is how it looks when written on paper:

"Write a melody in the assigned time-signature, using one Major scale of your choice. When the melody is ready, open *Soundtrap* and add the notes

---

9 *Soundtrap* is an online digital audio workstation that allows users to create music or podcasts, and to collaborate either with teachers, or in groups.

you composed. When you finish these two activities, create a libretto for your composition. Please look at the first row (4 bars) for an example in C Major."

A Collaborative Composition Project, and Necessary Steps when Explaining to your Students.

Firstly: I Instruct each student on how to create a free basic account and choose their username and password.

Then I have them complete a few questions on the worksheet I will have created for them before they signed up. I will use symbols from SoundtrapStudio.

An example: What is a DAW?[10] What is the music website we will be using? How do you collaborate with another student? Look at the image on the following page.

---

10 A DAW is a 'Digital Audio Workstation', a software application used to record, edit, and produce audio files.

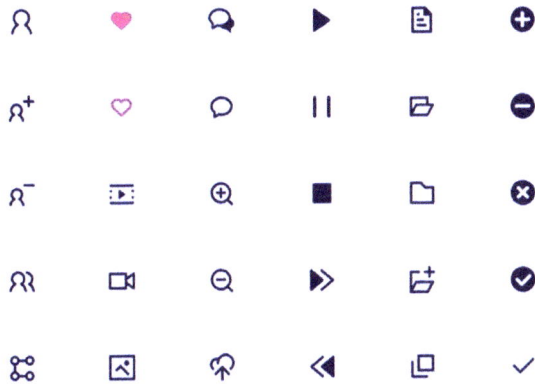

Why is it important to click this button often? (the *save* button), and more...

Secondly: I will have one student create a new project. That student should then invite another student to their project. I will have them experiment with how the changes they make are saved, and how the other person sees what they just did.

Thirdly: I will have them answer questions between themselves to determine who is in charge of which instruments and tracks. For this, I will create a template. After that, I will give them the assignments:

Student 1: You are in charge of the first four measures. Start at 1, and end at the beginning of measure 5.

Student 2: You are in charge of the second four measures. Start at 5, and end at the beginning of measure 9.

Then I will tell them about the design of the melody (I like to use 'design' as a word, as it is very diverse, and offers huge creativity and possibilities):

"Each section must include two loop tracks, but the loops should be separate from the drumbeats. Each unit must also have one drum, an instrument of your choice (strings or woodwinds), and a moments track, in which you will use the pattern to create a rhythm. Once this beat is created, it can be moved anywhere in your section. Moreover, it can be looped."

It is of great importance for my students to feel confident before I give them the collaboration project. If I want to continue this collaboration and make it a part of a Sonata or a Song for a musical, that will give me plenty of opportunities for more tracks and cooperation. I will always start with two or four measures.

Behavior-teaching Strategies, Developed Using Music, Art, and Composition.

Composing Using a Limited Number of Magnets, in the Style of Chess

This unique form of composition involves using magnets on a board to create musical phrases, similar to how chess pieces are moved on a board. It allows for a tactile and visual approach to music creation, which can lead to unexpected and creative results. Visual representation makes it accessible for different learning styles, especially for analytical students.

After the student has finished composing, he can be given a dry-erase marker in different colors if he wants to draw more notes, or to expand the composition. This way, we are not limiting the student's creativity: we are giving the student choice.

In the first part, when we are giving the number of magnets suggested by the teacher, we are teaching the student patience. Even though the number of magnets is limited, the student still has creativity on the music staff or blank board staff. When the student has used all the magnets and tells us he is done, then we offer more colors, asking the student if he wants to make any last-minute changes.

Why magnets from the beginning, and not dry-erase markers? Magnets are a more tactile and interactive tool for students to use, allowing them to move and manipulate the pieces physically. This can also help with fine motor skills and spatial reasoning. Dry-erase markers may not provide the same level of engagement or opportunity for hands-on learning.

But the journey continues during every lesson, with new chess composition ideas. The goal is to collect all of the boards and put them together as a single composition that will reveal itself. This way, the student doesn't have to do the whole composition in one hour, or on the same day: there is time for other activities as well, but the composition is creating itself with each lesson.

I also like to ask my students if they want to use the piano and hear each note, or if they want to close the piano, and hear and imagine the music notes in their heads. This helps them to be more creative and to develop their musical imagination, which is important for playing music with feeling and expression. It also allows them to explore different ways of interpreting the music and finding their own unique style. They are also training their ears at the same time.

This way of 'chess' composing is good for analytical students because it helps them develop their problem-solving skills and logical thinking abilities. Additionally, it enhances their auditory processing skills by training their ears to recognize patterns and sequences when analyzing the musical form or the harmony.

Compose a Song Using Numerical Years

We have to know our students' characters and strengths very well. Some students can be more mathematical. Allow the student to write or transcribe the musical piece or song using numerical years. Like 2021 pi. This method of transcribing music using numerical years is known as the "year numbering system", and can be a useful tool for musicians to communicate and share their compositions with others. It is particularly helpful when working with international students who may not speak the same language.

Why? It allows for clear communication and understanding between the instructor and the student, ensuring that the student is able to participate fully and succeed in the course. Additionally, it promotes inclusivity and diversity in the classroom.

By incorporating different teaching methods and materials that cater to diverse learning styles, the teacher can create a more inclusive and engaging classroom environment for all students, including those who excel in mathematics. This can lead to better academic performance and a stronger sense of belonging for all students. Mathematical students tend to have a logical and analytical mindset that allows them to approach problems in a systematic way. This makes them more comfortable with numbers than with language or artistic expression, and it will allow them to play the music and learn the piece in a way designed by themselves, in this case by using numbers.

Composing a Musical-theater Piece, or Chamber Music, using a story book

The student starts with one phrase at a time, and tries to compose or imitate an animal from the book that the teacher read aloud. It can be about any subjects or objects in the book (imagination, creativity, and expressions). This approach can help bring the story to life, and create a unique and engaging musical experience for the audience. It also allows for a range of musical styles and techniques to be explored, from classical to contemporary.

I have my student next to me at the piano. I open the book and start reading. The book I used to help the student create a musical was *Somewhere in the Meadow*. I will start reading a few sentences, and ask the student to compose the melody for the frog, or the melody for the fish. Then, after we've written all the notes for the different animals, we will go over the tempo, and here I will ask the student: "What is the tempo of the frog? The frog jumps, so let's make this staccato for the style"; or "What is the tempo of the fish? The fish flows, so let's make this moderato for the dynamics." Then we add instruments. "What kind of instrument are the frogs?" I ask my student. I let him tell me what instrument he associates with the frogs. "Who can be our singer?" "The bird," they say. "What about the crickets?" "They can represent the violin in our composition." Then I will go ahead and ask, "Ok, so now let's see how many bars of the frog or the crickets we have?" They will go and look at how many are in the picture, and add that to how long our musical phrase should last.

How can this benefit the students?

This exercise can benefit the students by improving their ability to count and keep track of musical phrases, which is an essential skill for any musician. Additionally, it can help them develop their visual perception, and attention to detail.

Over in the meadow, in a snug beehive,
Lived a mother honeybee and her little honeys five.

Composing a Musical Composition: a Piece Using Sentences and Words

This method uses language as a place to start thinking about music. Each sentence is turned into a musical phrase or motif. The resulting composition can be a unique blend of the spoken word and music.

Not all students are comfortable with the traditional way of writing music, which is to know the notes, harmony, and chords. What if the chords could be letters from the sentence? This approach is known as the "letter chord" method, and it allows students to create melodies without any prior knowledge of music theory, making it a great option for beginners, or for those who want to experiment with a new approach to song-writing. They can focus on the overall structure instead of being blocked and overwhelmed by all the technical details of traditional composition. This way of composing is great for students who are hyperactive, but who are also shy, and believe they can't compose. It's profound to experience how a student immediately gets interested in learning music by simply asking, "Which sentence would you like to compose?"

Then the student says, "I'd like my song to be called "Shopping Bag." Remember, first we must ask the students for the sentence, because he knows which music letters he knows well, and so is comfortable playing it on the piano or violin afterwards.

In this case, we used the words "shopping bag." Our musical notes were the letters from the words and their variations.

BAG (for 'bag') followed by GAB (the first word reversed, read backwards), and then we had repetitions of BAG and GAB.

Sometimes the sentences can be simple, sometimes long. It all depends on the level of the student—is he or she a beginner or an advanced student? Which strings and fingering does he or she know to play, on the violin or piano? We must take everything into account before we create the sentences.

There is another example where sometimes we might need to add additional letters to the keyboard, basically creating new notes with new letters: that is possible. We just create. It's our piece, it's contemporary, and it's the future of composing.

Look at this example:

The song was named *Bite of Venom*. We didn't have the letter "N" in the musical alphabet, so we decided to write it down on the piano and name the sound. Here again, I asked my student, "Which of the notes would you like to use for N? Do you prefer do, re, mi, fa, sol, la, ti, or do?"

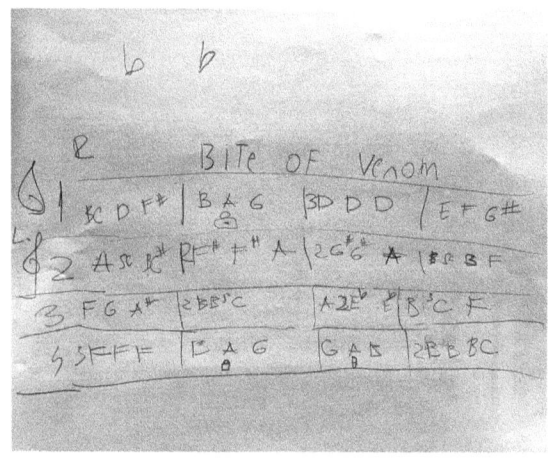

Visit the gallery for more examples

How to Learn to Play with Both Hands in Just One Lesson

In this lesson, with my beginner, I used *Morning Mood* by Edvard Grieg.

We started with one hand at a time.

We don't play with the right hand: we sing its music, playing only with the left hand; and then we play it the other way round.

We start by singing loudly, and each time we practice, we sing more quietly, until we hear and sing the music only inside our heads. This way, gradually, we teach the brain that the left or right hand is ready. Then we apply the melody of the left hand in the mind, but the left-hand fingers are playing the melody floating above the keyboard; and then slowly we put them onto the keyboard.

This is a good way for the student to practice dynamics in the song, as well as slowly transitioning towards the blending of the two hands together. By practicing this technique, the student can improve hand coordination and dexterity, which are essential skills for playing more complex pieces. Additionally, it helps the brain to develop a better understanding of how to divide tasks between the hands.

Additional Tips to be Used with the Above Methodologies

These are some additional tips I have created to enhance the lesson and make the structure more creative.

But first let's look at the structure: the lesson plan with the tasks to be checked.

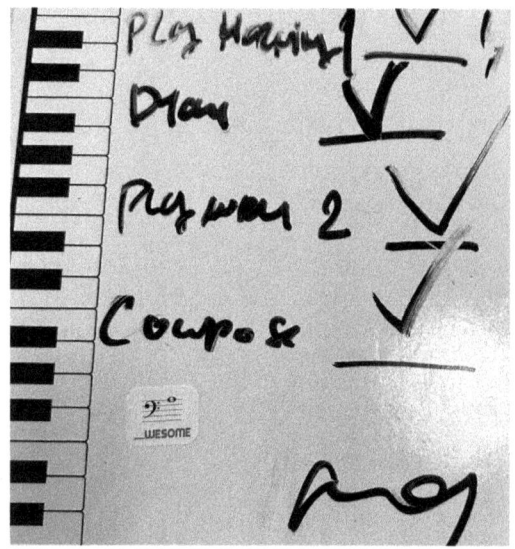

Lesson Structure

The lesson schedule, or the 'bus' as I call it, has four stops.

First I always introduce techniques like scales, and the first part of the song. I also like to divide their composition into two parts, in combination with other activities, as I feel they get the most out of the lesson;

having to draw, and to compose in between, keeps their attention.

The *second* task is to draw, and listen to the musical piece they are practicing.

The *third* task: they play the song.

The *fourth* task is to compose, and then play the song they have composed.

Notes and Rhythm

Let them write the letters on the note (so they can better read them). Once they are comfortable with the letters, introduce them to the concept of rhythm and how it relates to music. Encourage them to tap along to a beat, and eventually to try playing simple rhythms on an instrument.

---- Incorrect rhythms to improve articulation and correct the rhythm in the song and Etude to strengthen the hands

When I see and hear my students struggling to play a passage or just reading the music with the correct note value and needing the strength in their fingers, I have them practice each complex phrase in four ways, and then the fifth way would be the one that the composer writes. By using incorrect rhythms, the students are forced to focus on the articulation of

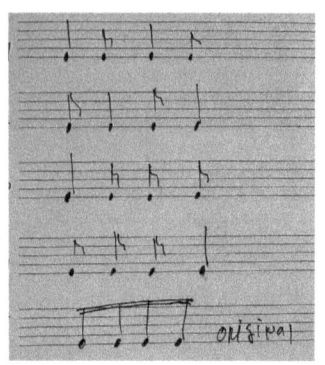

each note, which can ultimately improve their overall playing. Once they have mastered the incorrect rhythms, correcting them to match the composer's intended rhythm will come more easily. It also challenges the player to think outside the box.

To develop a good sound, sustained bow strokes, and an even vibrato, when I work with my violin

students on introducing different musical bow expressions, which are forms of musical articulation like détaché, martelé, spiccato, staccato, and ricochet, in various combinations and at other places on the bow, I always use the violin etude from Kreutzer's Study No. 1

This etude is an excellent tool for developing bow control and coordination. It also helps students understand how different bowing techniques can affect the sound and expression of the music they play. The repetitive notes and the more they practice help them develop calluses that protect the fingertips on the left hand. By practicing these techniques in the context of a musical piece, students can develop their skills while improving their overall musicianship.

Another etude I want to give to piano beginner students to help improve the strength of the fingers in the left and right hands is Schradieck Exercise No. 1 on one string. I ask them to play this etude for this exercise, slowly starting and buildinzg the tempo. From 60 to 120 on the metronome. This exercise helps the students improve their finger dexterity and accuracy and trainsthe to increase their speed while maintaining control gradually. It is a great way to develop their technical skills and prepare them for more challenging pieces in the future.

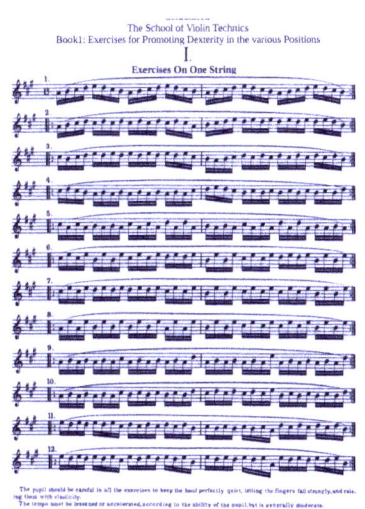

Soft, Loud, and Medium Music Dynamics and How to Use Them

Teaching children about soft, loud, and medium music dynamics can help them understand how to use different levels of volume in their rhythms, and create more dynamic and expressive music. It can also improve their listening skills, and their ability to identify different levels of volume in music. They don't even have to play the piece to hear the dynamics; based on the direction in which the notes are moving, either 'upstairs' or 'downstairs' (as I tell them), we add the medium, loud, or soft dynamic. These loud, quiet, soft, and medium can replace the traditional dynamics names like forte, piano, pianissimo, crescendo, decrescendo, or mezzo forte.

Learning the Strings on the Violin or Viola

Learn the G-string, then compose a song on the G-string. Learn the A-string, then compose a song from that string. By the time you've completed learning the 4 strings and composing the 4 songs, the student knows the letters and the notes. This approach to learning can be a fun and creative way of engaging students in the learning process. It allows them to explore their musical abilities while also developing their literacy skills. It can also boost their confidence as a violinist, on their violin journey.

Look at the picture.

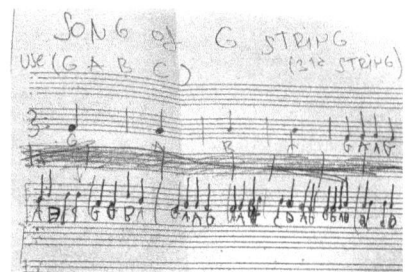

Copy and Paste

Have them write the song they are playing (or paint the song)—it speeds up the process by having them learn the notes visually instead of in the traditional way. This technique is particularly useful for beginners who may struggle with reading sheet music. Additionally, it can help students develop their creativity and interpretation skills by encouraging them to visualize the music they are playing.

History and Listening Development in Music for Beginners

This is particularly important for beginners, as it can help them understand the context and meaning behind the music they are learning, leading to a deeper appreciation and enjoyment of the art form. By your incorporating historical and cultural elements into their music education, students can also gain a broader understanding of the role music plays in society.

(They draw the composer, starting when the song starts, listening to the song, and drawing until it finishes.) Teach them to be patient, to follow, and to focus. This exercise not only helps to improve their drawing skills, but also enhances their ability to concentrate on a task for an extended period. It can also be a fun and engaging way to introduce children to different types of music and composers. It can help them with the ability to multitask.

Ready, Set, Go!

How to help the young beginner pianist start using both hands while learning.

1. Have the letters written on the piano keyboard, in two octaves, one higher and one lower.

2. Have the music open on the stand.

3. Tell the student that the notes in the treble and bass clef are twins, or best friends, and that they like to play together, at the same time.

4. On READY, have him or her find the right-hand letter in the treble clef; on SET, have him/her find the left-hand note in the bass clef; and on GO, have him/her press with both the left and right hands together.

This exercise will help the student understand how to read and play notes simultaneously in the treble and bass clef--essential for playing piano music. With practice, the student will become more comfortable playing with both hands, and reading music in multiple clefs.

Assignments and Exercises

Assignments and exercises suggested and developed for this book, and for my teaching method

Chapter 1: Assignments

Please pick one technique and one school of your choice. (The instrument technique doesn't have to be from the school you have chosen.)

Step 1

Write down the strengths and weaknesses of your chosen school and technique. When doing this exercise, consider your student's culture, and hands, and the state of his or her current left- and right-hand position and foundation. You can take a picture of the hand position while the student holds the violin, and examine it visually.

Step 2

Now write down your student's strengths and weaknesses while he or she holds the violin and plays with the right and left hand.

_____

_____

Step 3

Create different techniques

1. With your student's strengths, and the strengthof one or two schools

2. With your student's weaknesses, and the weakness of one or two schools

3. With your student's weaknesses and strengths from the school

4. With your student's strengths and weaknessesfrom one or two of the schools you picked.

5. Ask your student if you can create a new technique for him or her.

If your student agrees, write your newly developed technique here.

_____

Now that you have finished this exercise, think about how the origin of the school and/or technique you chose will affect the culture and background of your student.

Write down:

The Pros: _____

The Cons: _____

What are some music pieces that you could give to your student to play?

_____

_____

_____

Are you going to select pieces from his culture?

_____

_____

Are you going to compose a piece for your student?

_____

_____

Would you ask your student if he would like to write his own song to play?

Answer here:

_____

_____

_____

What do these cultures have in common, and what is not part of your student's culture? Will this affect his or her hands and physical structure? Will that affect him or her emotionally when choosing the proper technique or making/changing the foundation of their hands?

Take a moment to think.

Chapters 2 & 3: Assignments

Step 1

Ask your students to pick a country representing one of the techniques and schools.

Step 2

Ask your students if they have any preferred composer from that country; if the students answer 'yes,' write the name down; if the students answer 'no', ask if you can play different songs, and ask them to tell you which one they connect with. Which one provides peace for them? Which one motivates them? Now ask how they are feeling at the moment.

If they are stressed, give them the piece that calms them and ask them to analyze the music piece comparing their character, emotions, and memories.

If the students lack motivation or feel blocked, give them another piece that improves their productivity, and let them repeat the exercise.

Before all of this: given the option, would your student rather take a walk in nature and 'listen' to the exercise?

(Remember, your student might feel they need more time to feel ready to do the assignment. That's why we are providing this option.)

Another option, in addition to this, is to let your student record his/her answer using audio instead writing it down in his/her journal.

Remember that your student might be better at accomplishing the assignments by either using recorded voice for answers, or a written paper.

The Health of your Student

If you feel that your student needs more energy and is feeling tired or burned out, try to connect your student with the nutritionist at your institution; or if the nutritionist is unavailable, refer your student, or let your student read the theory of nutrition and explore or create a nutrition plan that makes him/her happy. Good nurturing equals a feeling of happiness.

Well-being and health are essential for the performance by, and success of, your student.

Before we go on another assignment to create for your student, let's think of you: your health as an educator; educator and student; educator, parent ,and student; or simply someone who wants to become one of these in the future.

Assignment for You

For better performance emotionally and physically, and your creative brain.

Please take a moment during your break, or whenever possible, to write or record these answers.

How are you feeling today?

Can you teach the lesson today?

Are you feeling overwhelmed?

Do you still listen to music as you used to in high school and college, getting ready for your degree?

Reading the chapter on the composers and their creative styles and feelings, do you recognize any of those habits--in your childhood, or growing up? For example: I have the temperament of Mozart. Oh, I remember that I had the same striving for perfection that Beethoven had! Or you remember the same situation that happened in their lives, that caused emotions to flourish, either sad or happy; and that in that period, they composed their most accomplished and famous pieces.

One exercise for you

Try to see what was happening in Mozart's childhood, and his diagnosis. How would you have helped

Mozart to feel better, and manage himself better? Which piece from another composer would you pick for him?

Try to learn more about how their music was written and how they felt then—the strength and weaknesses of their musical compositions.

Answers here:_____

_____

_____

_____

Now back to the student assignments!

Chapter 4: Assignments

Step 1

Exercise 1

List four composers, and their compositions, that use repetitive movements. Try to pick musical pieces that differ in style, and are different periods.

_____

_____

_____

Now

Read this excerpt about different types of composing; you can use any of these styles to recreate them, or combine them with the existing techniques. The last and most creative option is to ask your student to look at the composition (visually) and pick different bars that he would like to put into a song. This way, you will see what his/her perception of music is, using their eyes and what is pleasant for their vision. Then ask the student to try to hear the melody in his/her mind before choosing the different bars. You will be amazed at how the composition will sound at the end. It might be the piece that could be transformative for the student's success and emotional well-being.

The Fragment:

composing in

Augmentation

Music composition by augmentation refers to creating a new piece of music by expanding on an existing melody or theme. This technique allows composers to explore variations and possibilities while maintaining a cohesive structure.

Imitation

Imitative composition can be rigorous, with precise repetition. It can be free; it can be artificial. And it can be repeated after it ends.

Composing using Imitative composition is a helpful tool for learning and practicing different writing styles. It allows writers to experiment with other techniques and structures, ultimately developing their unique voice and style.

Look at examples here:

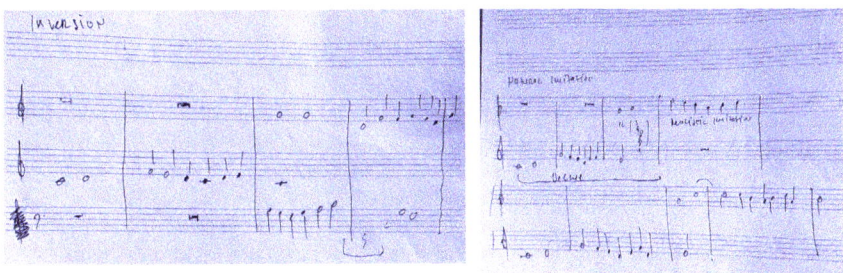

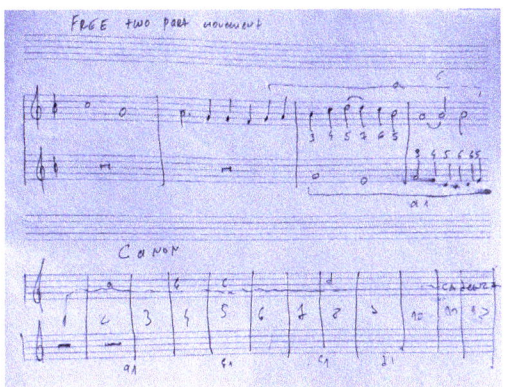

Step 2

Ask your student about the different expressions in the composition of Bach's toccata and fugue, Mozart's Symphony No. 40, or others.

Questions to ask:

Does it sound: Flamboyant, jocular, comfortable, calm, arbitrary, restless, melodious, gentle, cheerful, recitative, angry, heroic, resolute, at will, stately, free-paced, boisterous, weepy?...and you can add more here

Step 3

If your student is more prone to listening:

1. Play the recording and ask the student to take notes of the time when he/she hears these expressions and what he/she feels. Let him/her take notes.

If your student is more prone to visuals:

2. Ask the student to circle the places in the composition, using different colored pencils, to express and note the different expressions.

Step 4

Ask to perform the now composed or recreated song, together with your student.

Have your hand on his/her/their hand or have him/her/them only play with the left hand while you play the right hand, if the piece has both bass and treble clef, or if it's a piece with accompaniment.

Chapter 5
Inclusion Diversity--Your Voice--the rights

I imagine your classroom has students from different cultures around the world.

Exercise 1

Step 1

Ask your students to list the esthetics and aesthetics of their countries.

And their likes and dislikes.

Step 2

Ask your students to write two compositions based on one of their likes and esthetics and one based on their dislikes and aesthetics.

An Exercise: Let them work in groups to create a composition.

Put students from different countries together, and let them use the country's likes and dislikes to compose two pieces.

1. They can compose traditionally.
2. They can compose digitally.
3. They can give colors to the likes and dislikes. Ask them to hear the letters, and write it down visually, using colors for each like or dislike.

When they have the above compositions ready, ask them how they sound. If they were to change and improve their country, would that be helpful through music? Is that a way to fight for advocacy, rights, and inclusion?

If not, let them write down which way they think they can help to improve the issues discussed and mentioned above.

Another Exercise:

Ask them to create a definition of the word "School."

Ask them what different words/terms sound like to them.

Back to you.

Chapter 6

Exercise

You have four different painters.

Pick one and note an element from the image that makes you feel happy and complete: try to sketch that.

From that sketch, name your composition.

Then compose music, based on the name.

If you are also a teacher, do this exercise with your student using children's paintings, and reflections on famous painters.

In addition, beforehand, read this article here:

Kandinsky and colors

Chapter 7

Analyze your student here:

_____

_____

_____

What do you notice that makes him/her/them happy during the class?

Ask him/her/them how his/her/their friends are. Does he/she sometimes play music together with them, or to them?

Does he/she/they want to learn some new piece that would make someone he/she/they cares about happy?

_____

_____

How was his/her/their week?

_____

_____

_____

Discover together the piece he/she/they likes to learn; you will be surprised how much they can help in the process, when you want to adapt the curriculum and make it successful for them.

Personal Note

The standard curriculum often teaches us to diagnose the students' weaknesses to make them progress and succeed in learning. Let us be different, and focus on their strengths and likings. At least, these are my thoughts.

Chapter 8-------------***Your chapter!***

Welcome to your book and your teaching style. You are the right person to write my eighth chapter. I would like you to help me learn what I haven't covered in these chapters, which would contribute to the world of education everywhere around the globe.

Gallery of Images

Painting Composers **210**

Various ways of Composing Using
Mixed Combinations **234**

Lesson Tasks Developed Together &
Accomplished Individually **248**

Copy Paste Learning Song **254**

Assisted Various Tools for Different
Learning Styles **256**

Adapted Notation Using Mulptiple Methods
and Colors **270**

Composing on Paper **288**

Painting Composers

Franz Joseph Haydn
(1732 - 1809)

Ludwig van Beethoven
(1770 -1827)

Wolfgang Amadeus Mozart
(1756 -1791)

Antonio Vivaldi
(1678 -1741)

On Music Education, Psychology & Different Abilities

Hector Berlioz
(1803 -1869)

Robert Schumann
(1810 -1856)

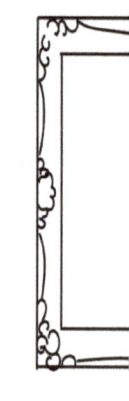

Gioacchino Rossini
(1792-1868)

Sofija Zlatanova

Giuseppe Verdi (1813–1901)

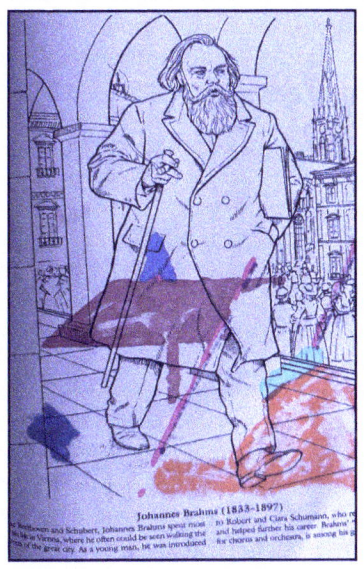

Johannes Brahms (1833–1897)

Johannes Brahms
(1833 - 1897)

On Music Education, Psychology & Different Abilities

Felix Mendelssohn
(1809 -1847)

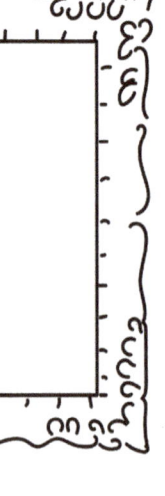

Felix Mendelssohn
(1809 -1847)

Edvard Grieg (1843-1907)

Edvard Grieg
(1843 -1907)

Gustav Mahler (1860-1911)

Scott Joplin (1867?-1917)

Claude Debussy
(1862-1918)

On Music Education, Psychology & Different Abilities

Arnold Schoenberg (1874-1951)

Austrian composer Arnold Schoenberg invented a new kind of music that did not rely on traditional harmony. He was one of the most original composers of the twentieth century. Born to a Jewish family, Schoenberg fled Nazi Germany with his wife and young and came to America. One of his most *Transfigured Night*.

Arnold Schoenberg
(1874-1951)

Jean Sibelius
(1865 -1957)

On Music Education, Psychology & Different Abilities

Wolfgang Amadeus Mozart
(1756 -1791)

Dimitri Shostakovich
(1906 -1975)

Various Ways of Composing Using Mixed Combinations

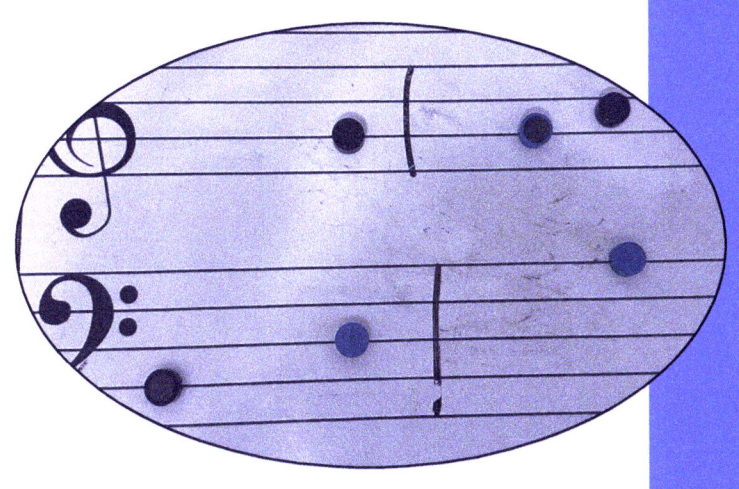

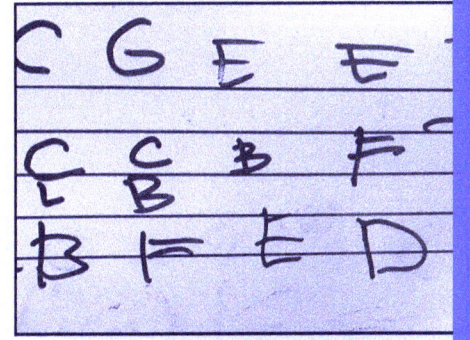

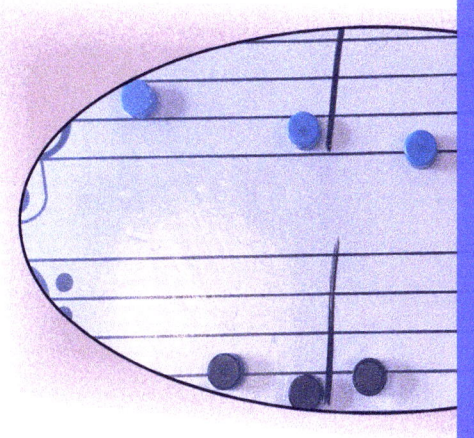

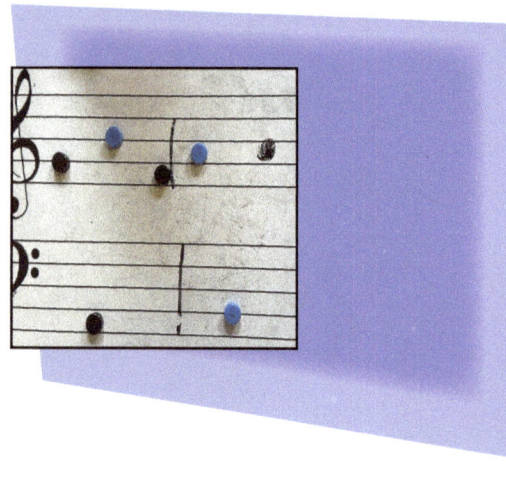

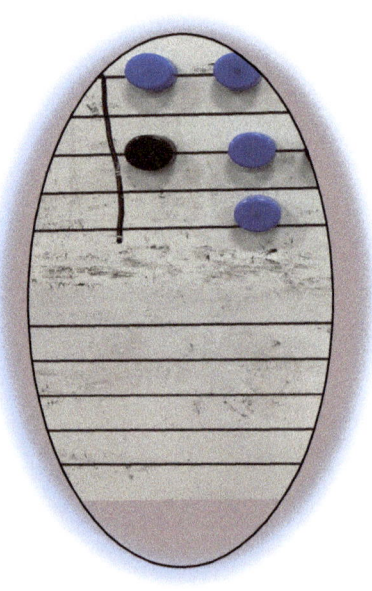

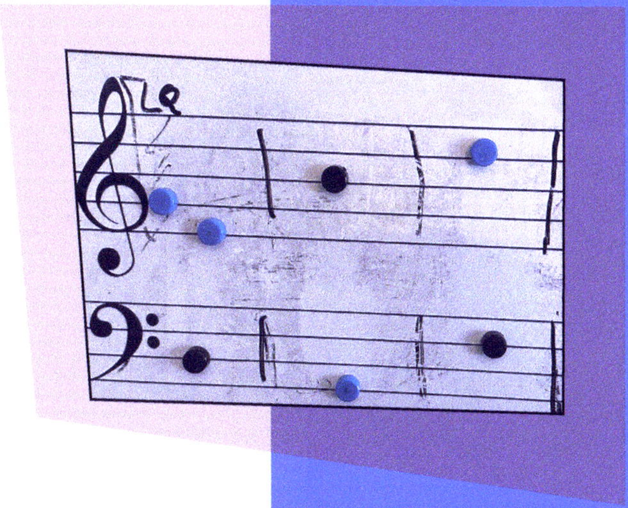

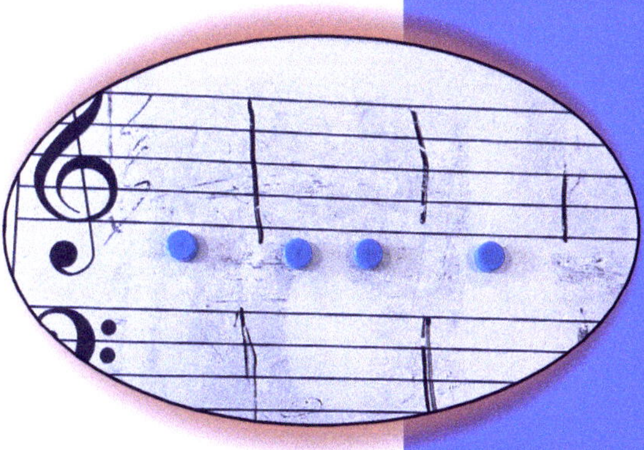

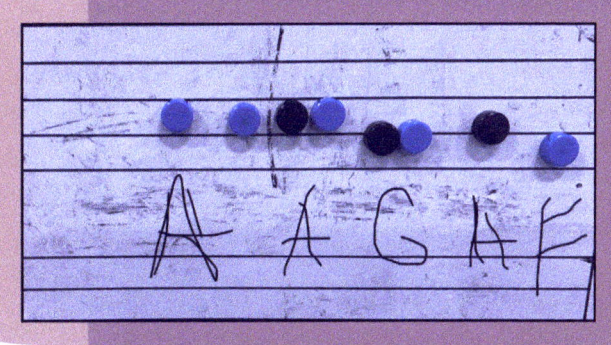

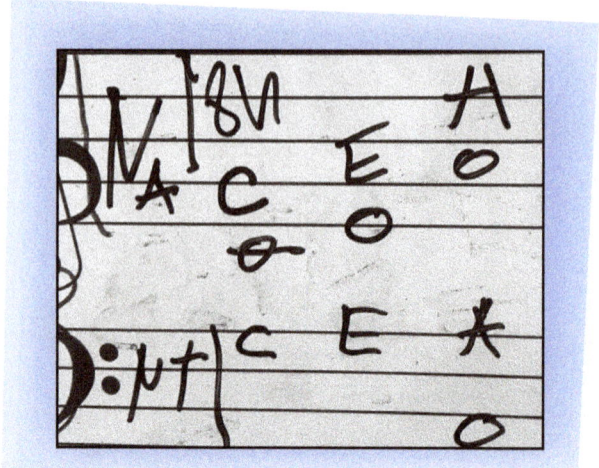

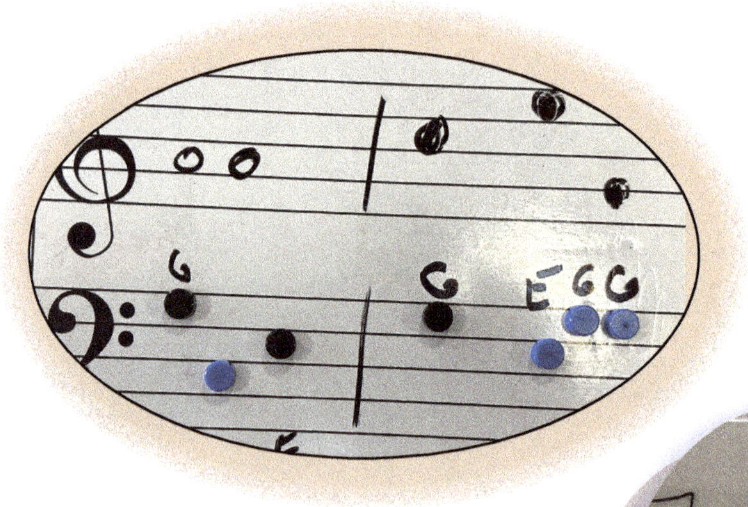

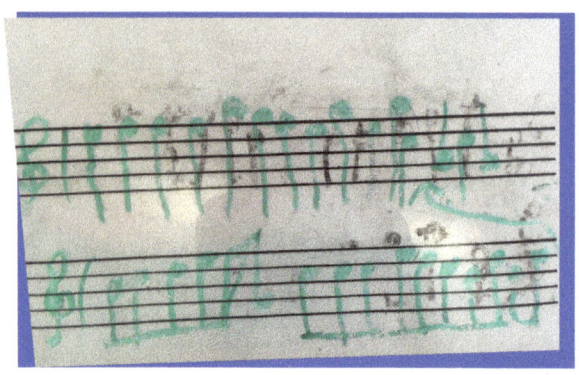

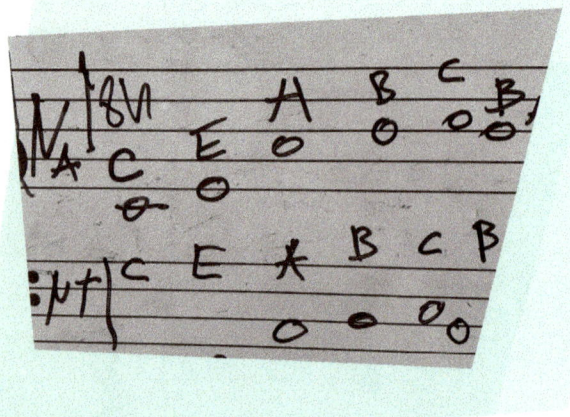

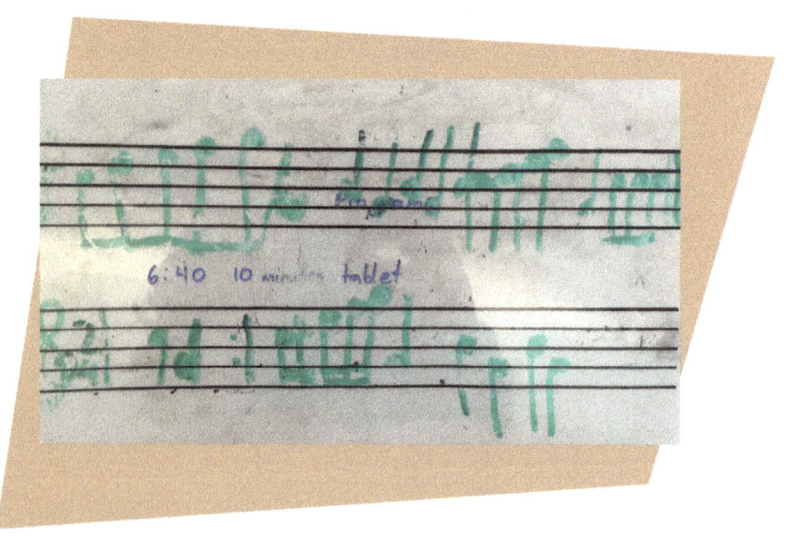

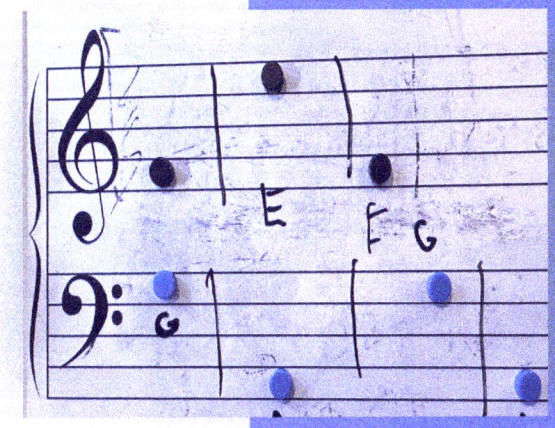
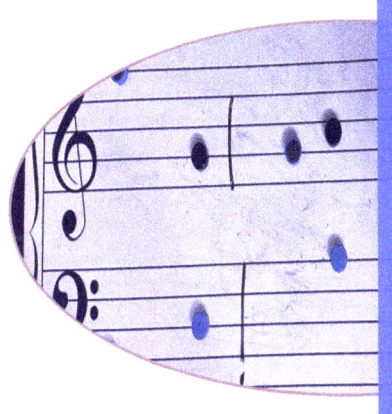

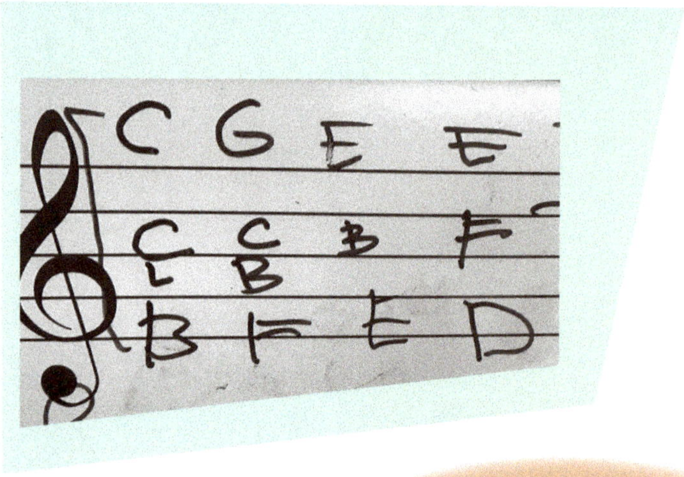

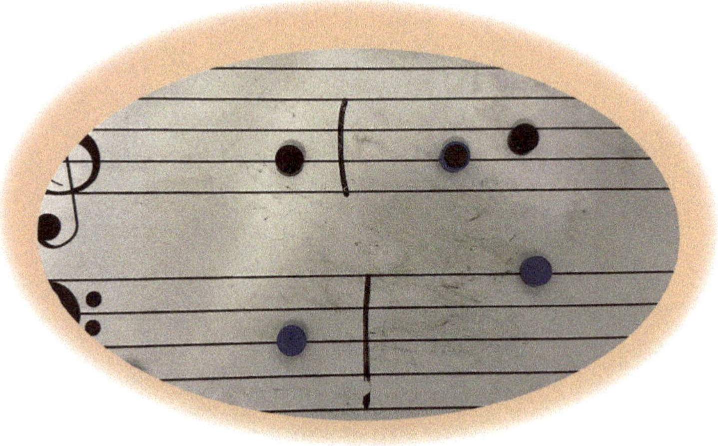

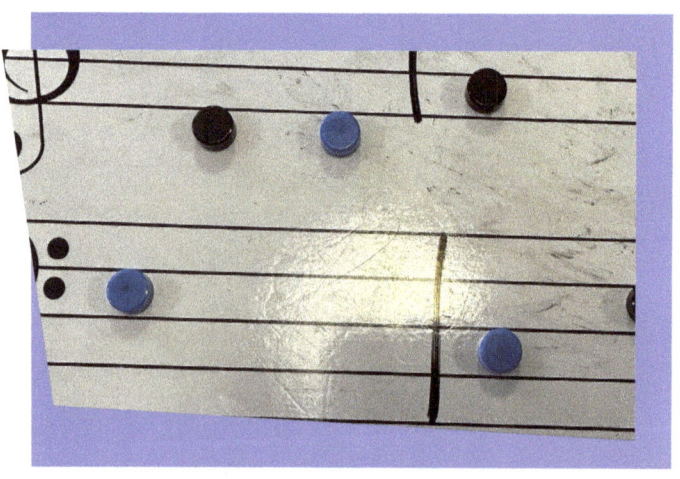

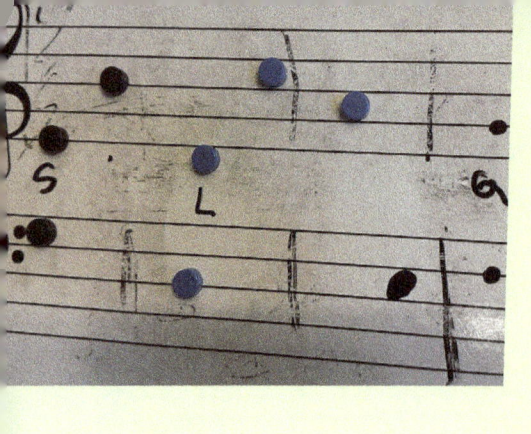

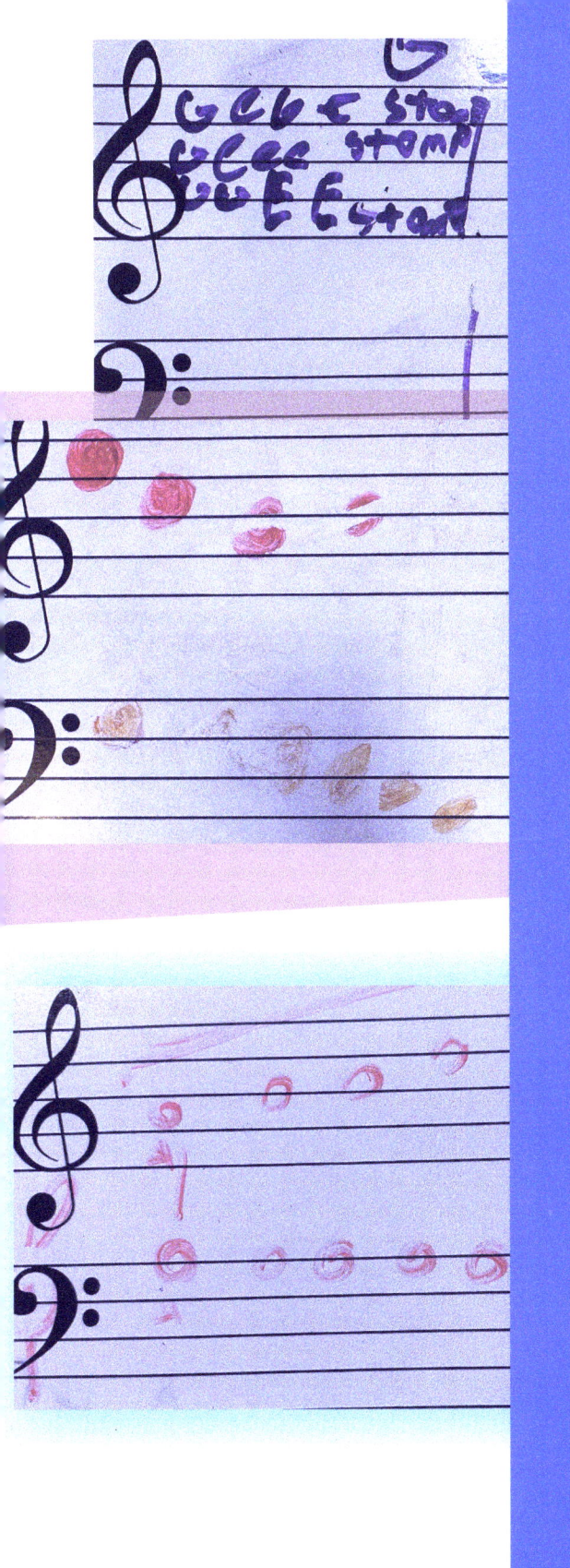

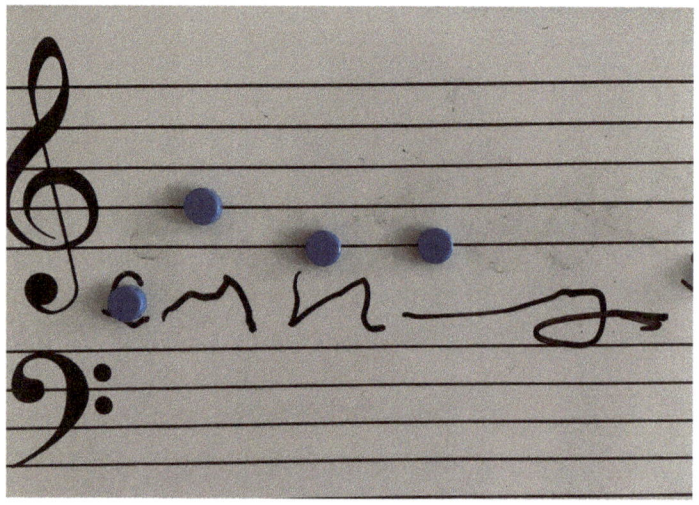

Lesson Tasks Developed Together & Accomplished Individually

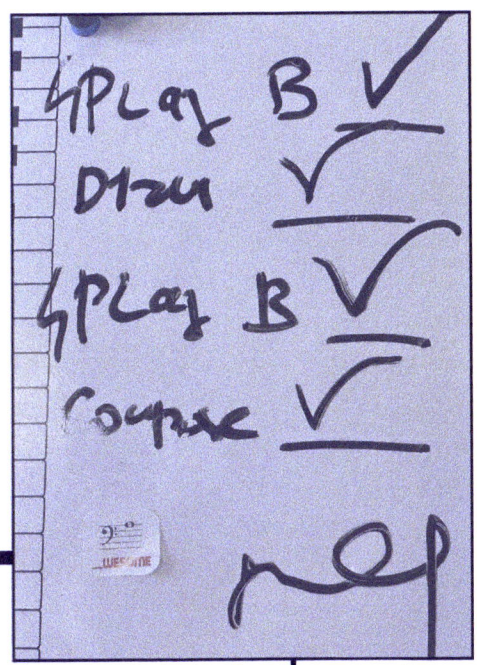

Sofija Zlatanova

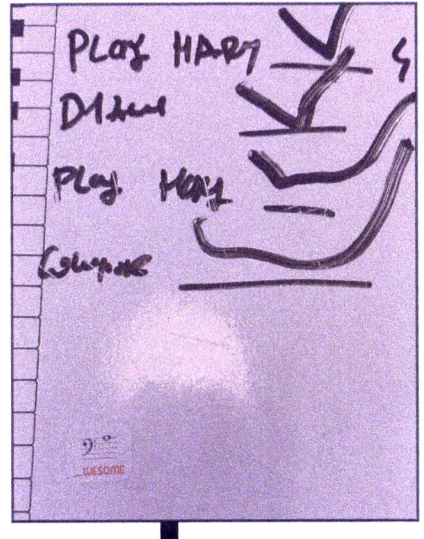

On Music Education, Psychology & Different Abilities

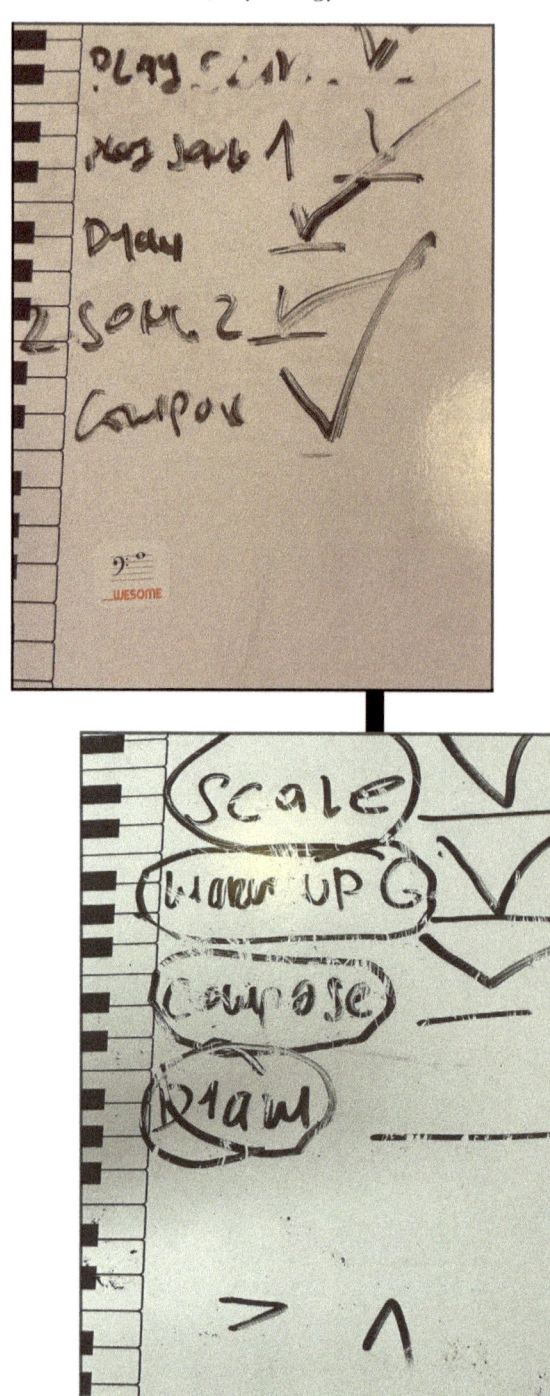

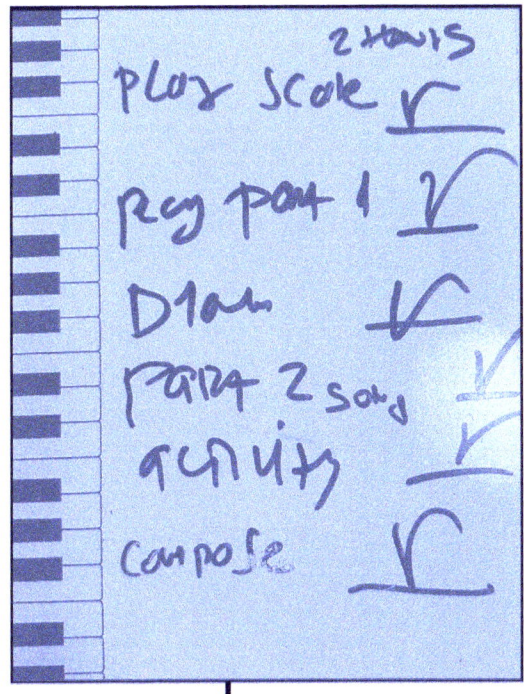

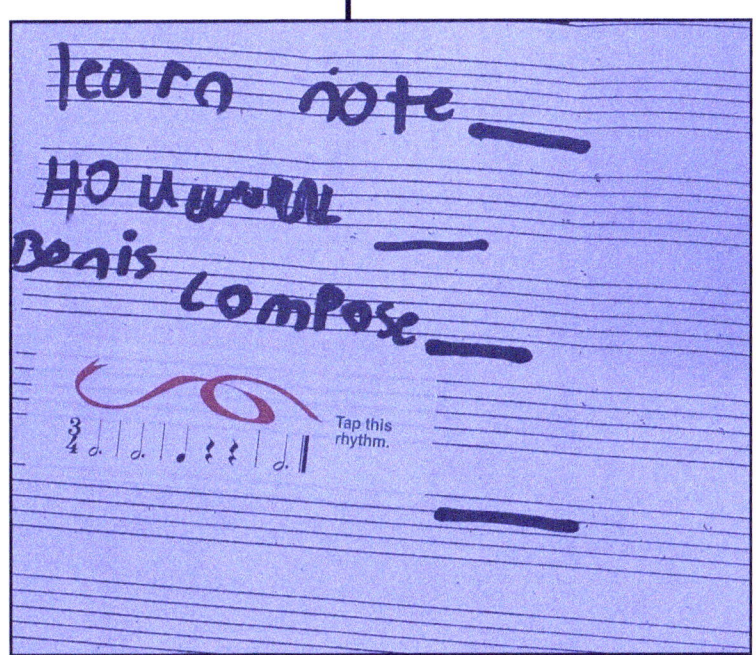

Copy Paste Learning Song

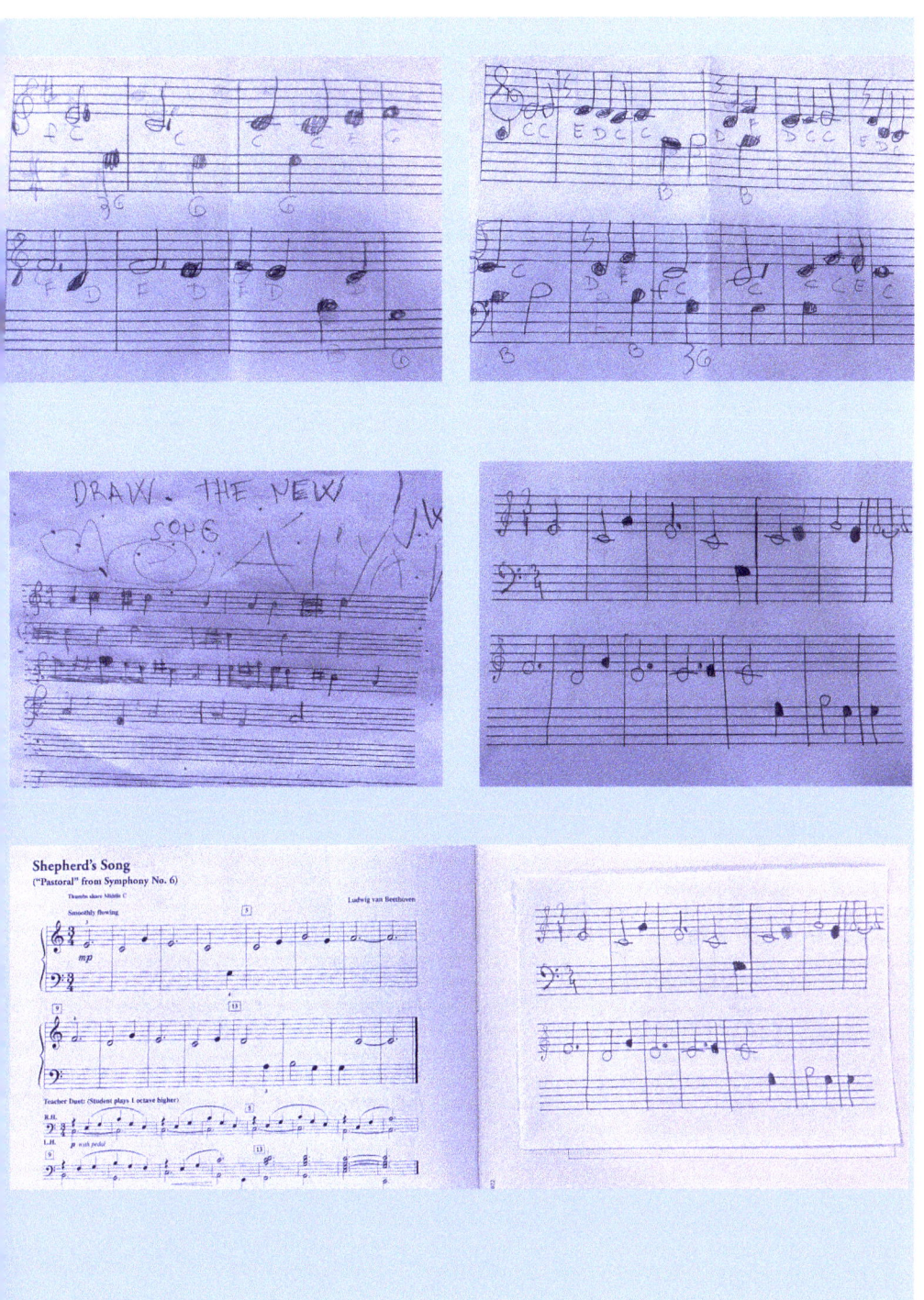

Assisted Various Tools for Different Learning Styles

"Buzz!" said the mother.
"We buzz," said the five.
So they buzzed and they hummed.
Near the snug beehive.

Over in the meadow, in a snug beehive,
Lived a mother honeybee and her little honeys five.

On Music Education, Psychology & Different Abilities

Sofija Zlatanova

Over in the meadow, in a nest built of sticks,
Lived a black mother crow and her little crows six.

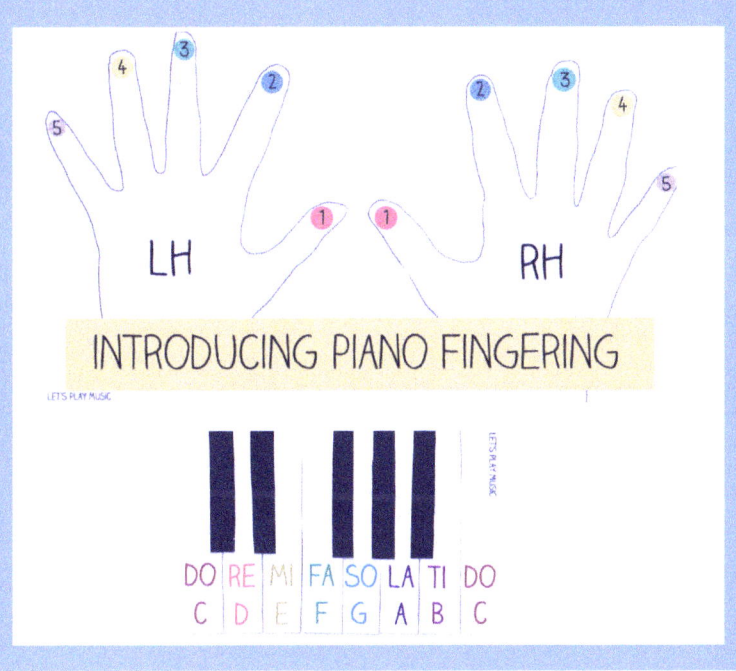

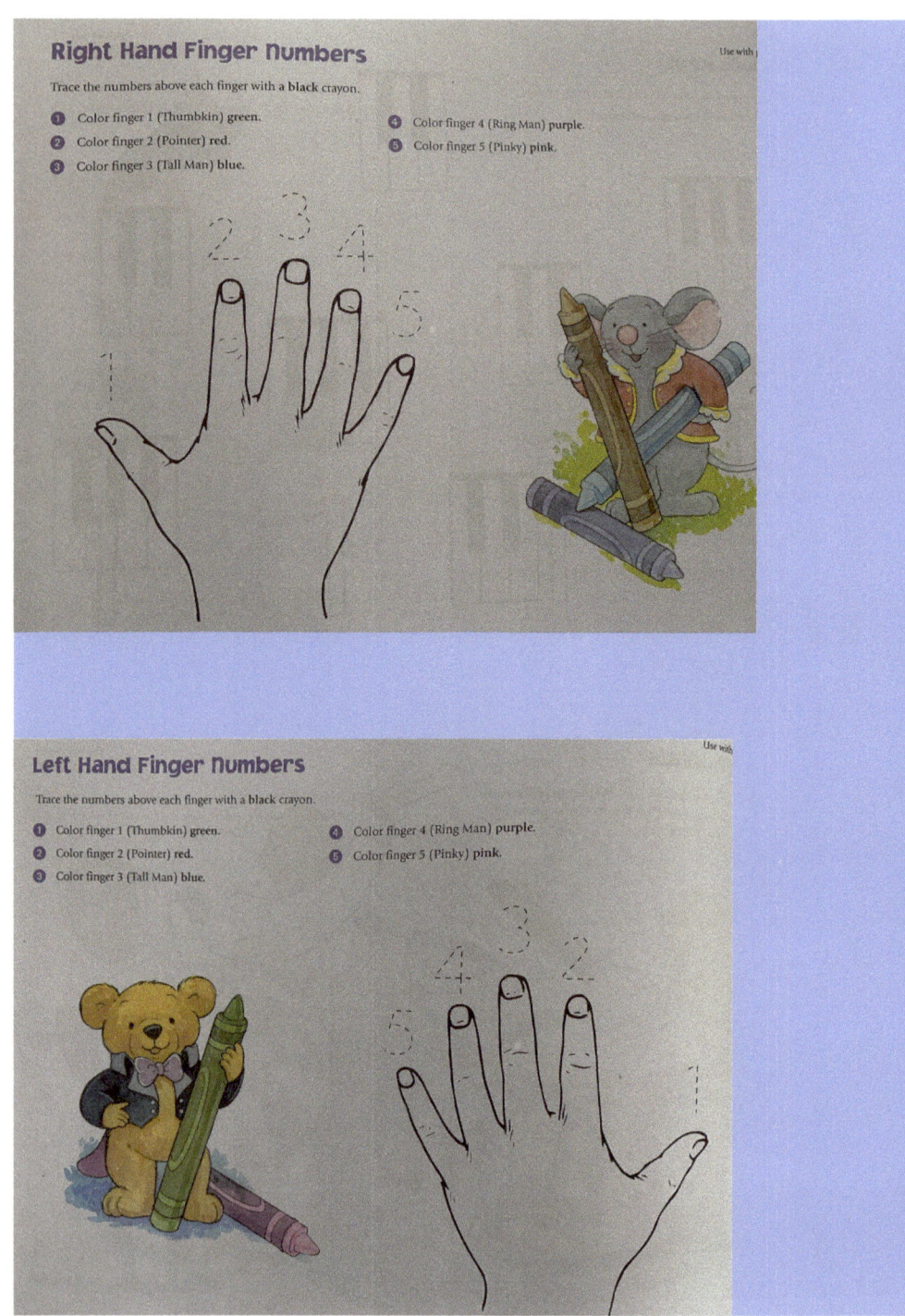

On Music Education, Psychology & Different Abilities

On Music Education, Psychology & Different Abilities

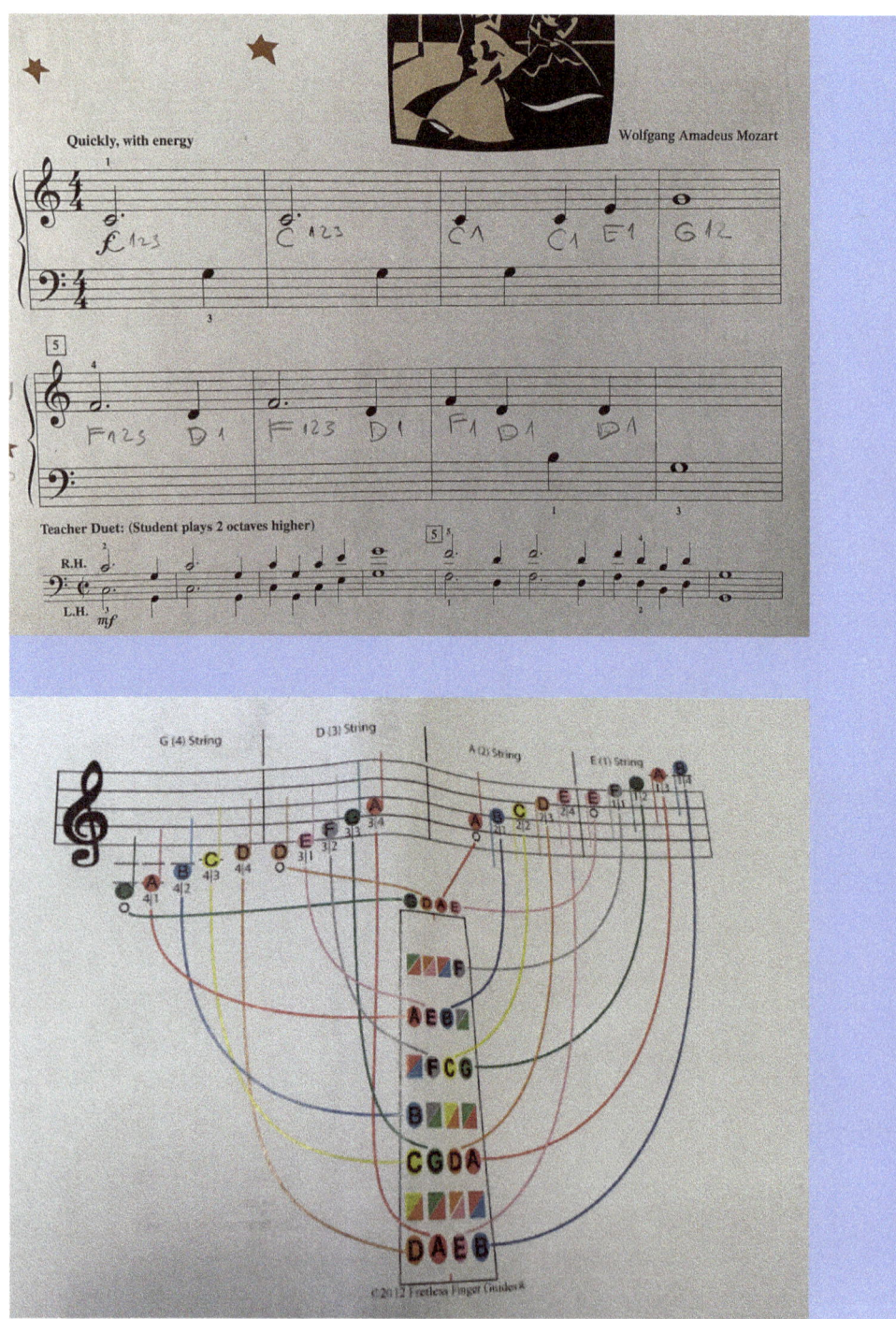

Adapted Notation Using Mulptiple Methods and Colors

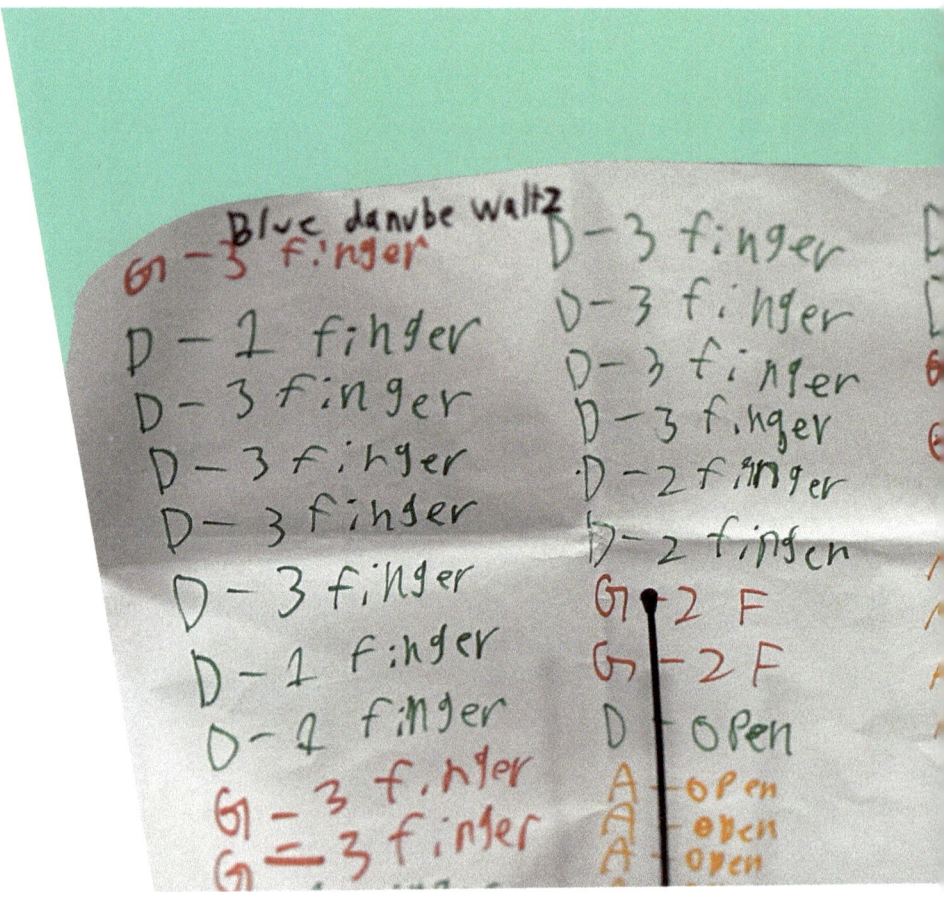

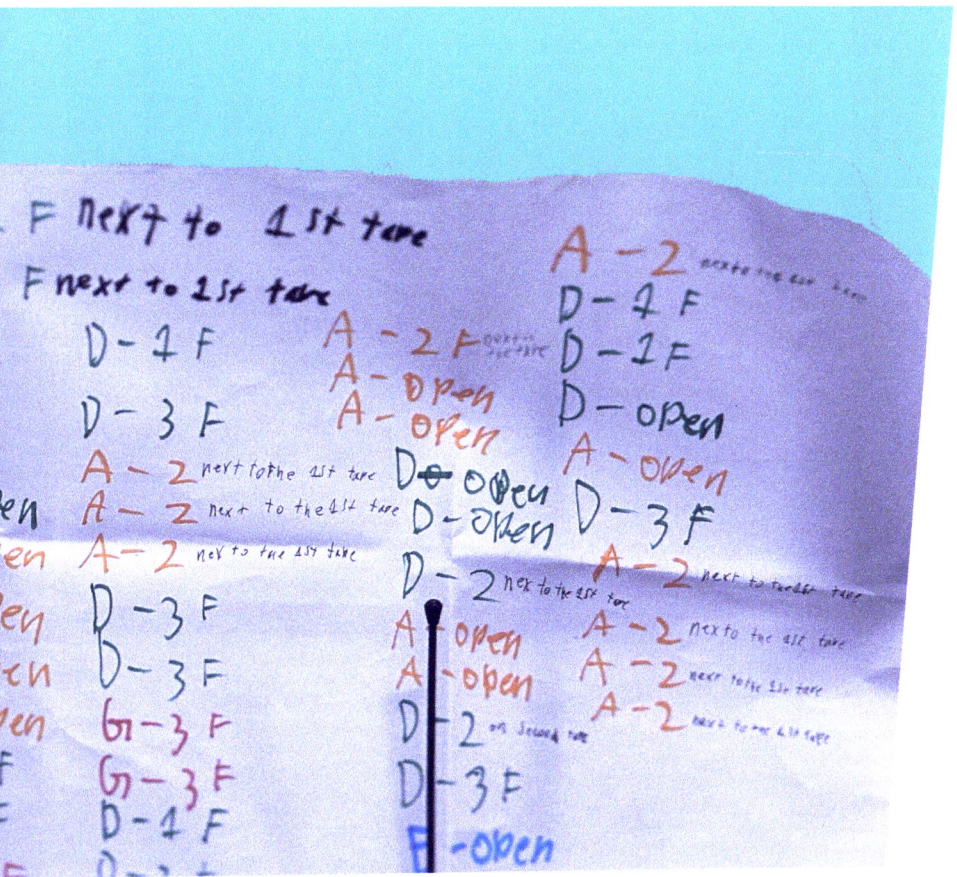

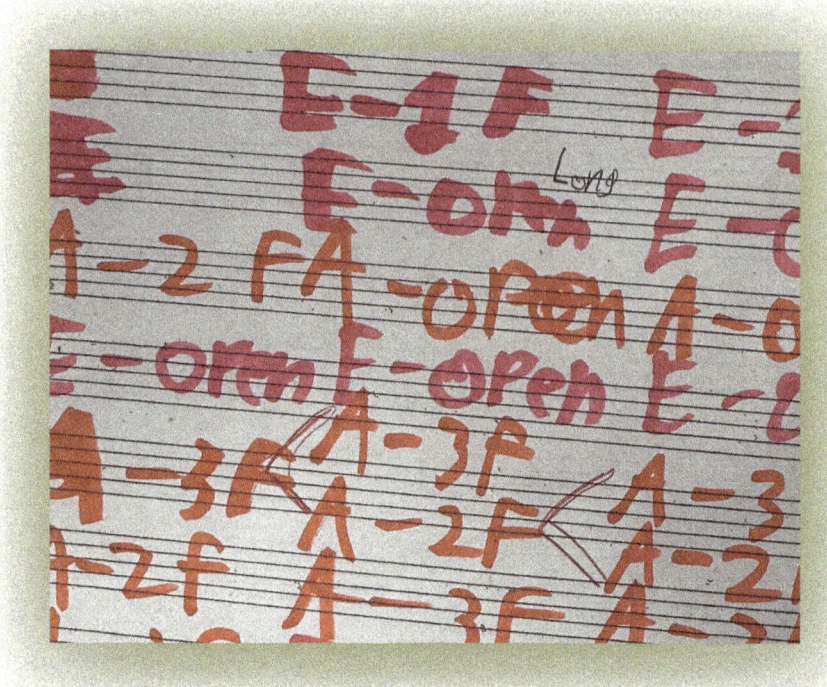

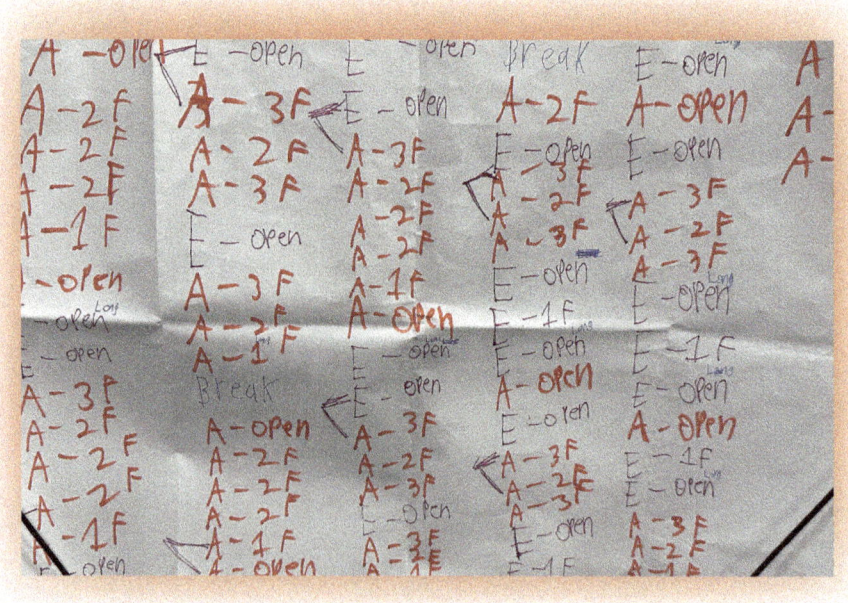

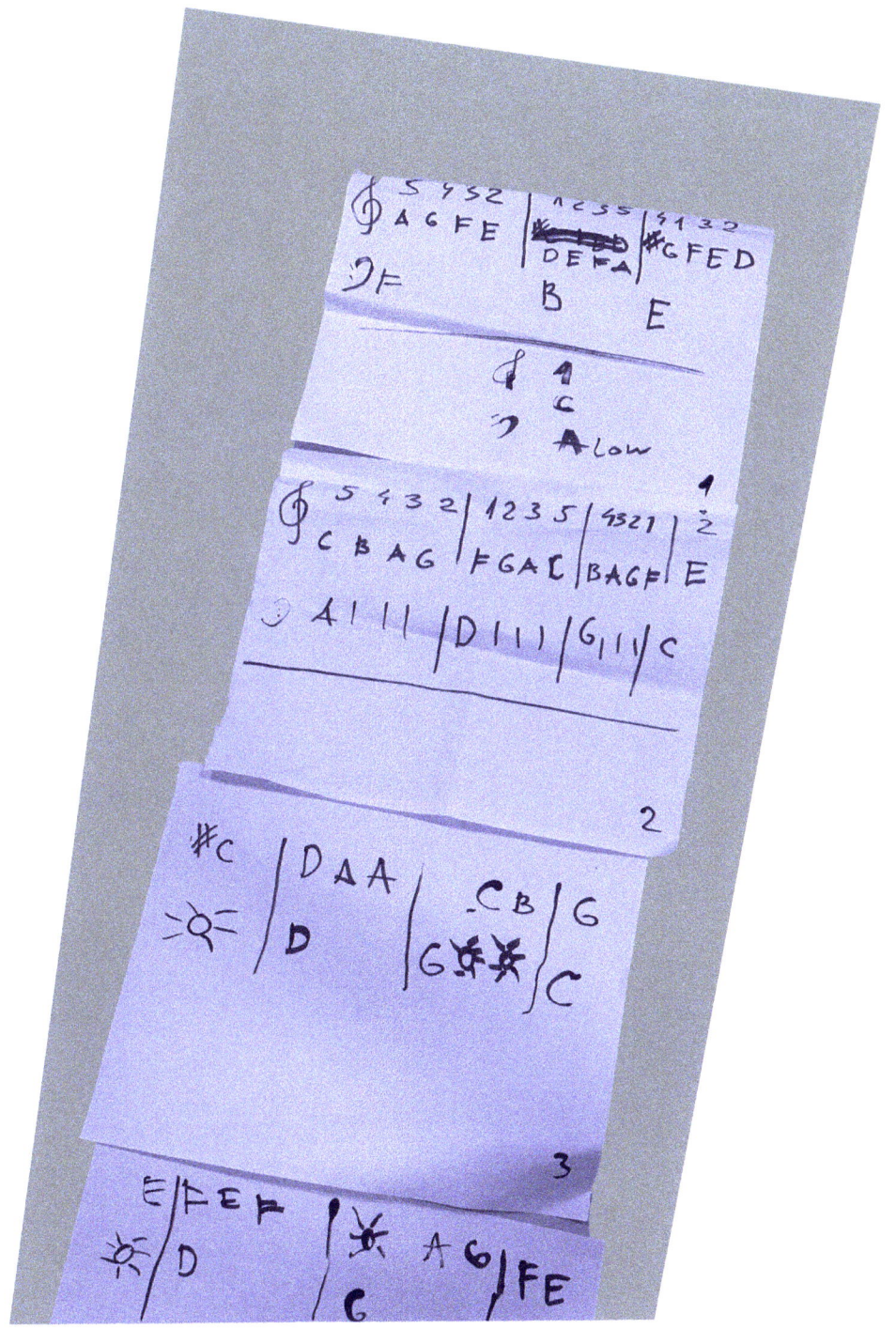

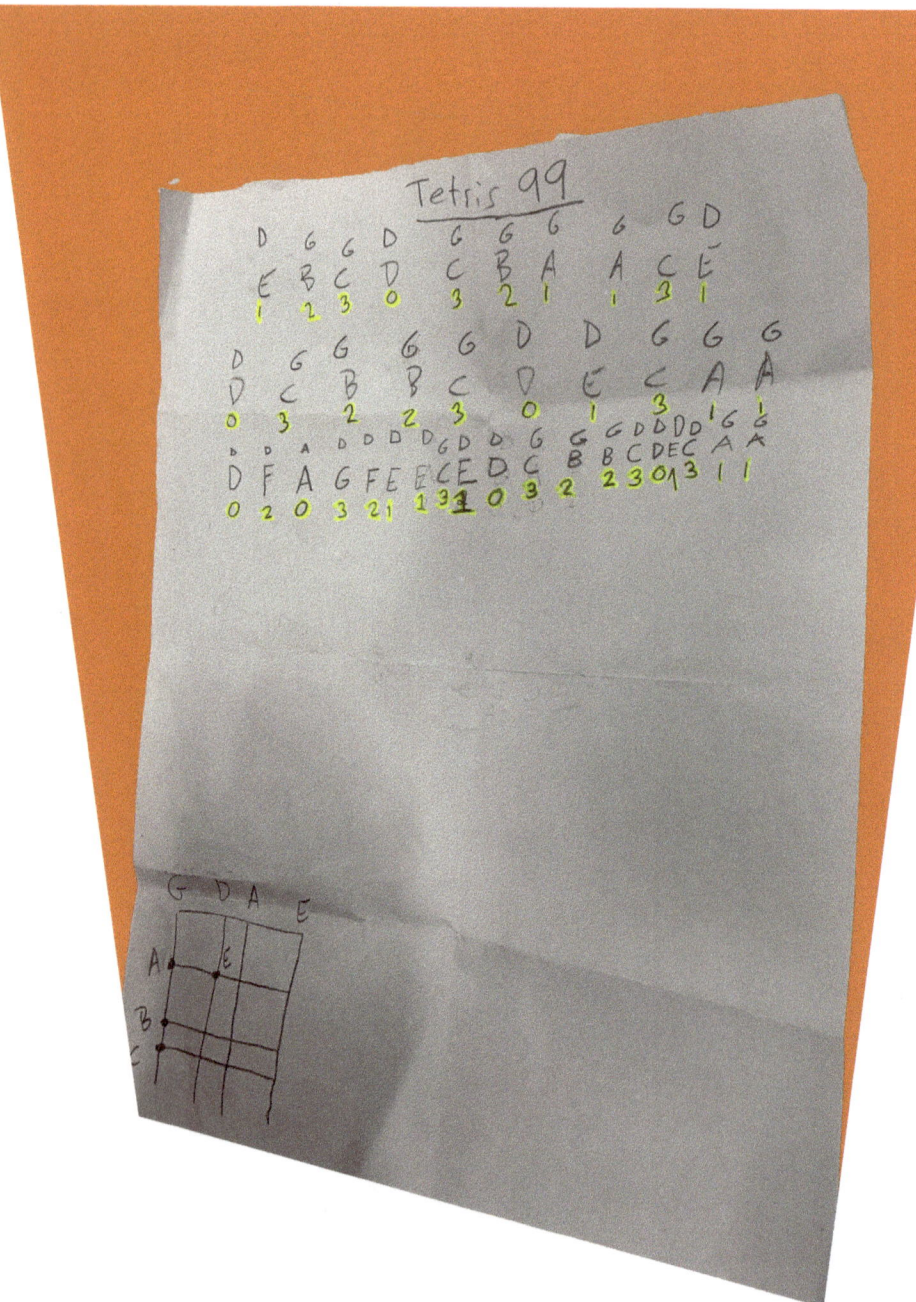

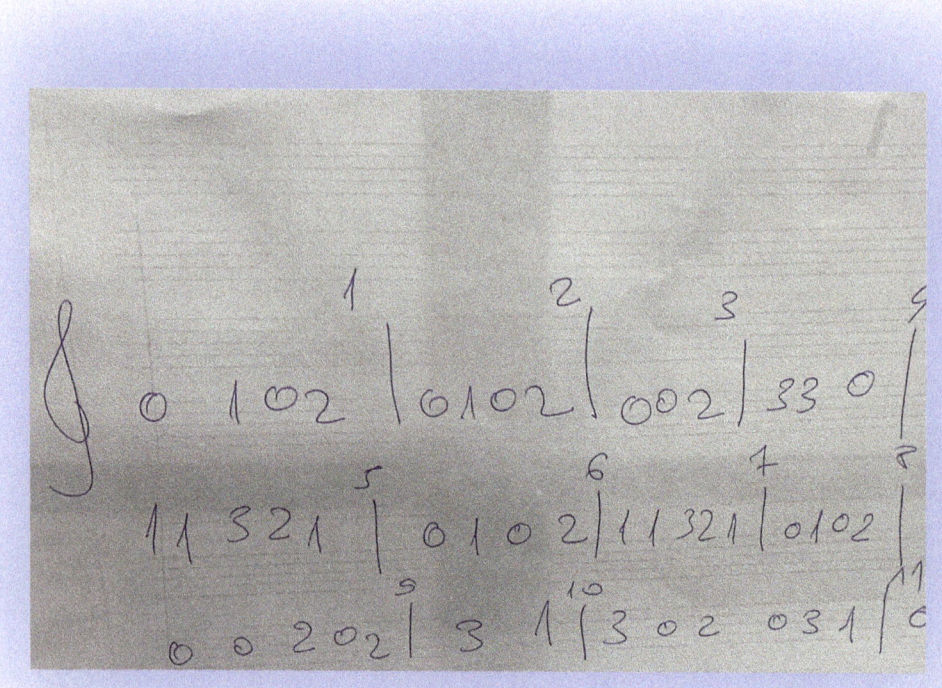

On Music Education, Psychology & Different Abilities

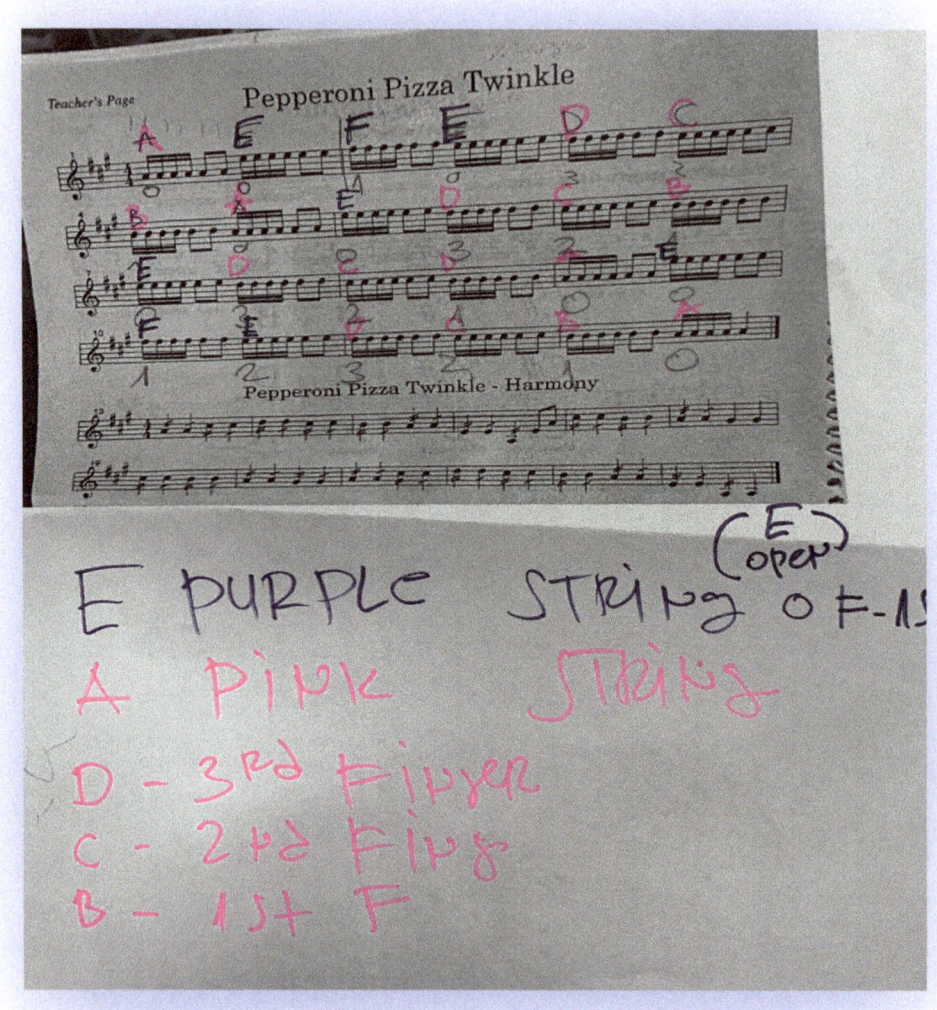

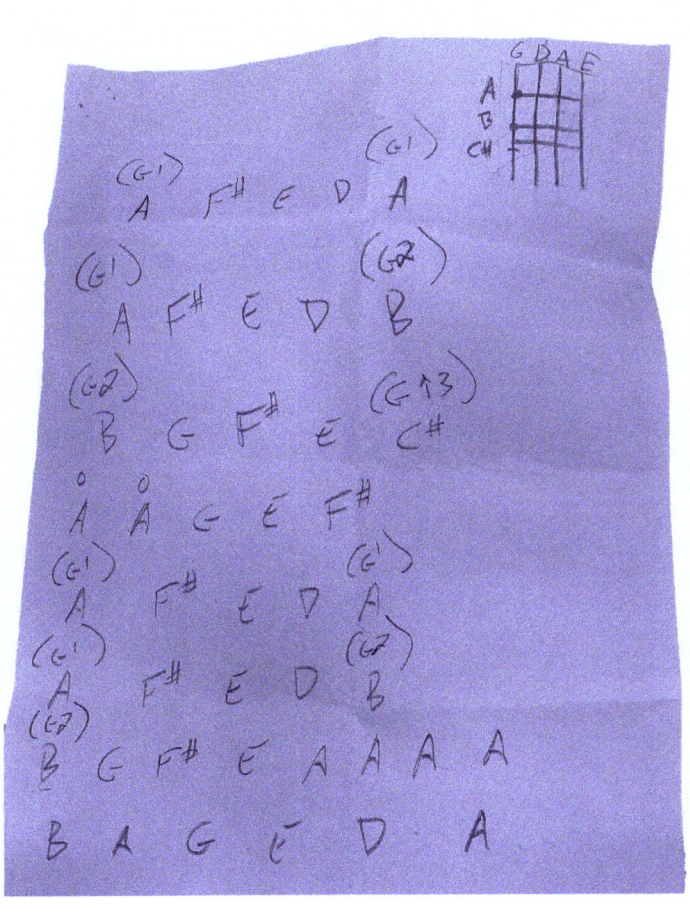

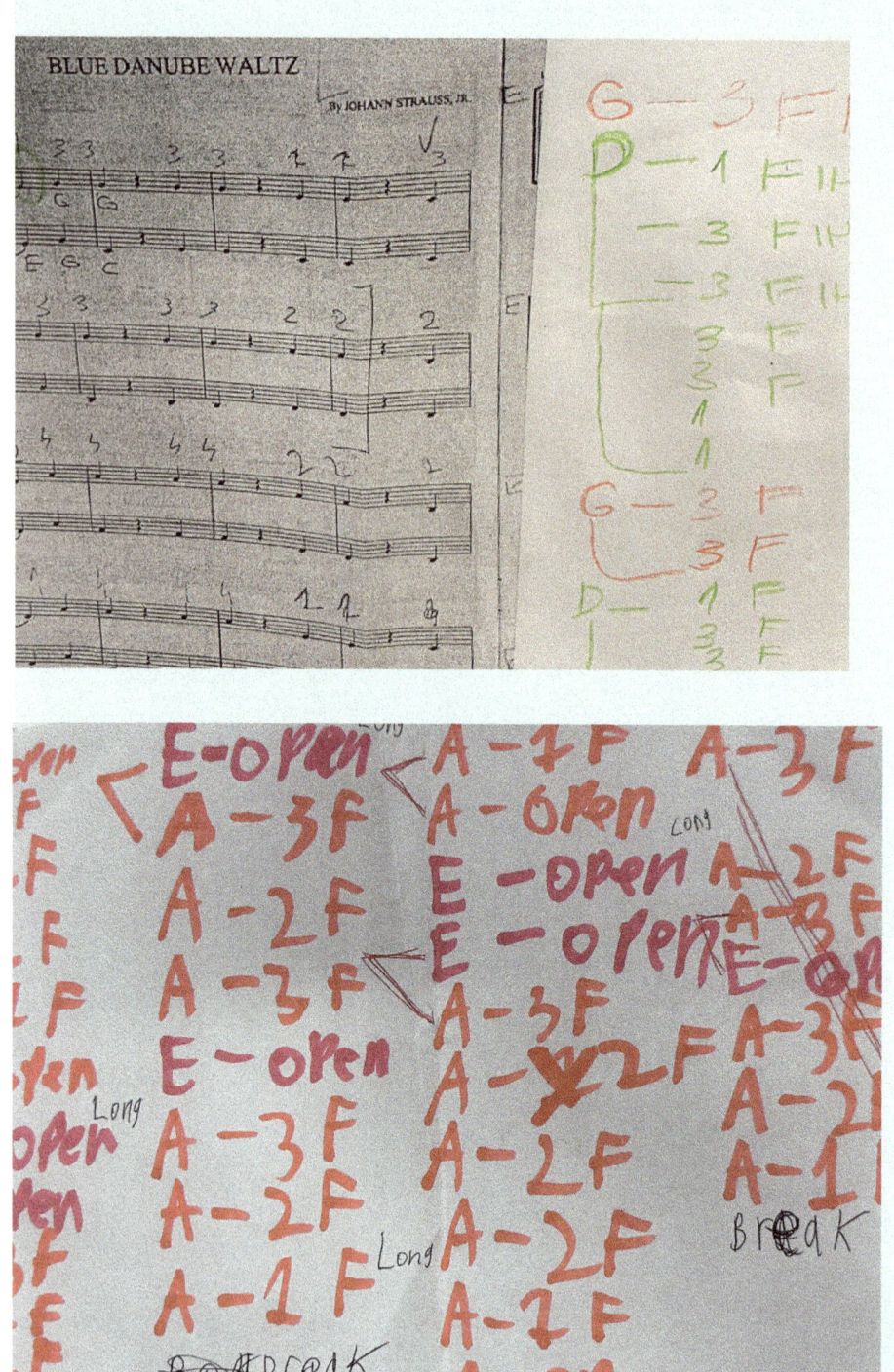

6.40 10

LINE
2 2 3 4 | 4 3 2 1 | 0 0 1 2 |
2 1 1 | 2 2 3 4 | 4 3 2 1 | 0 0 1 2
1 0 0 |

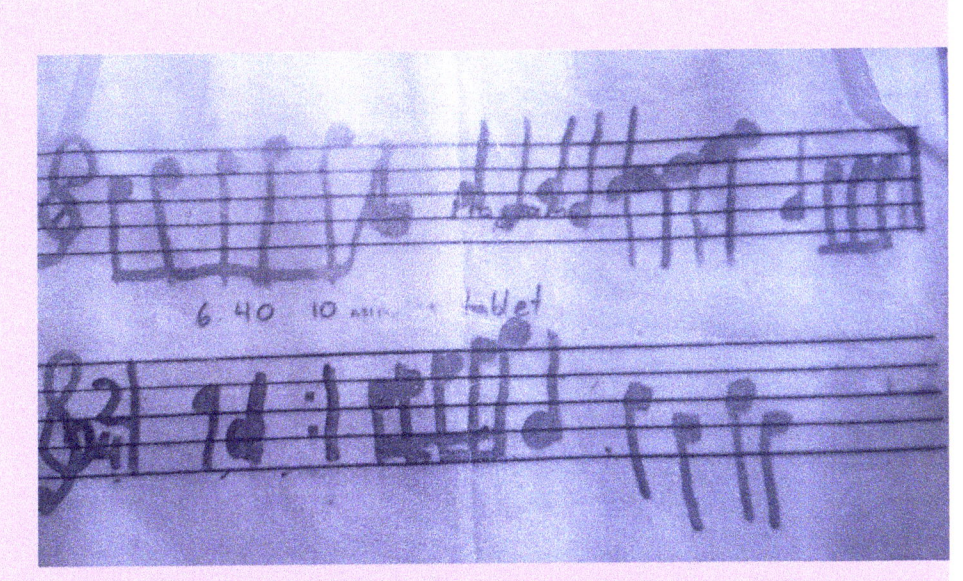

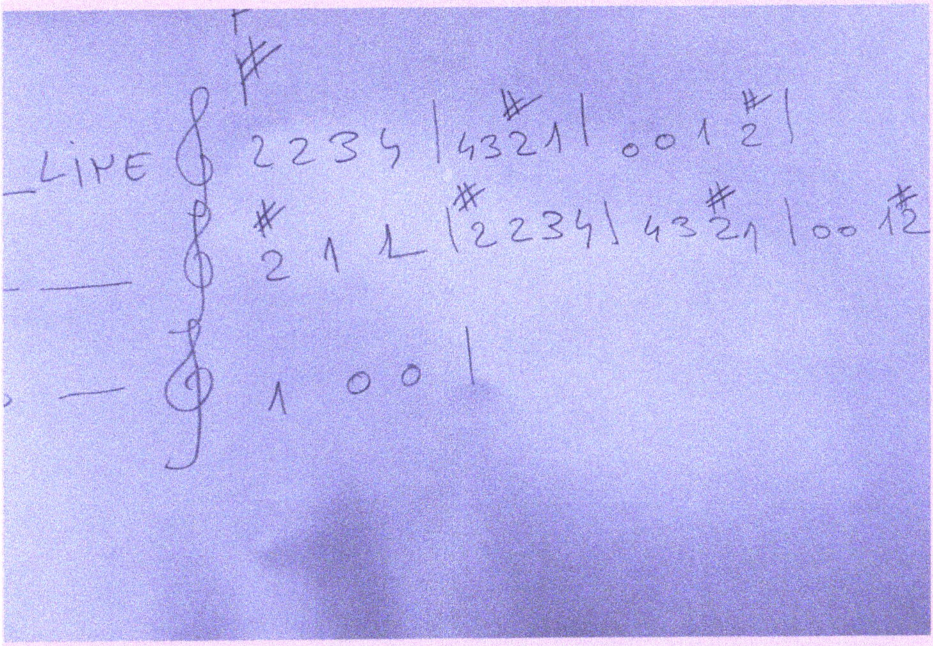

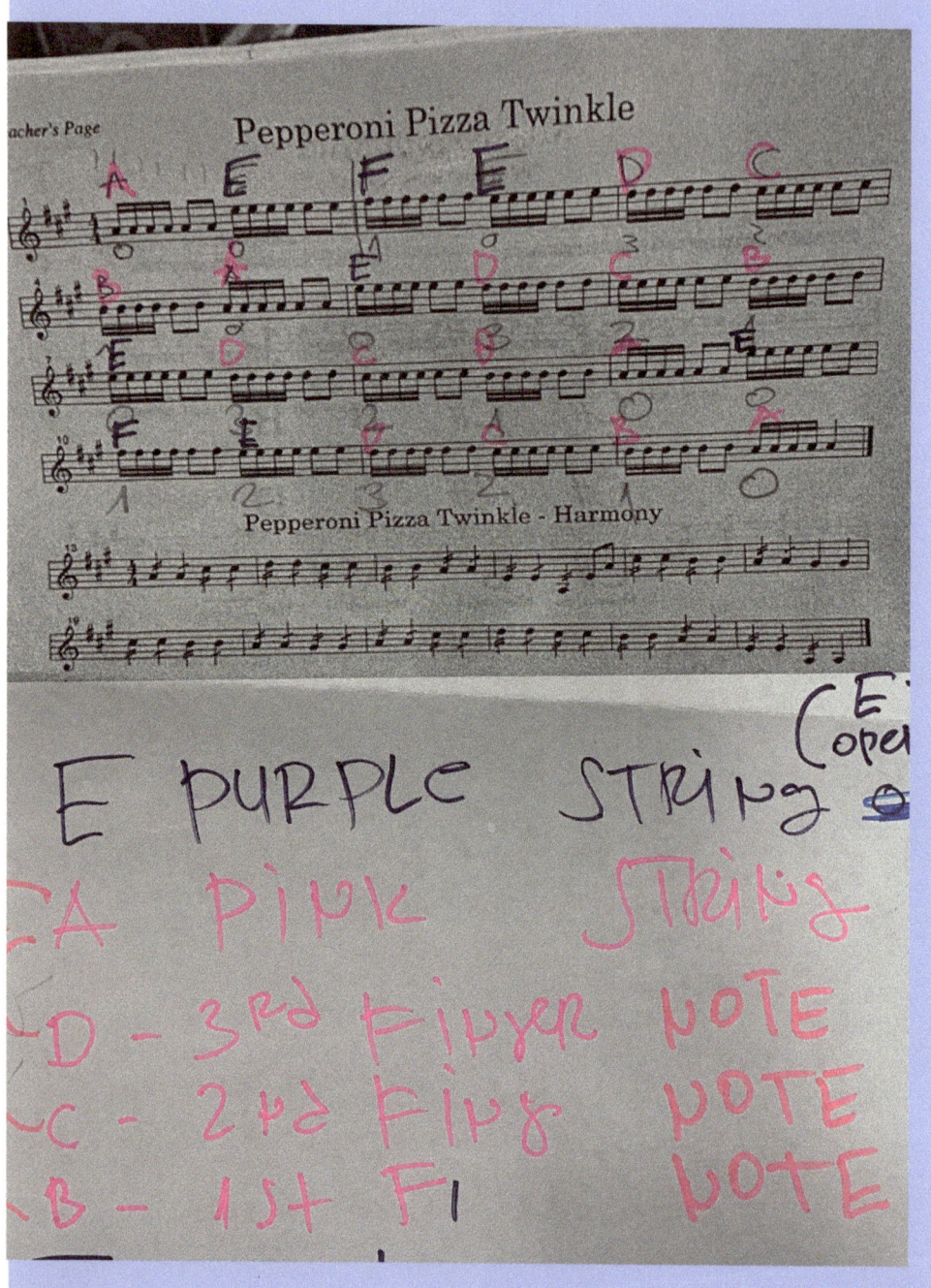

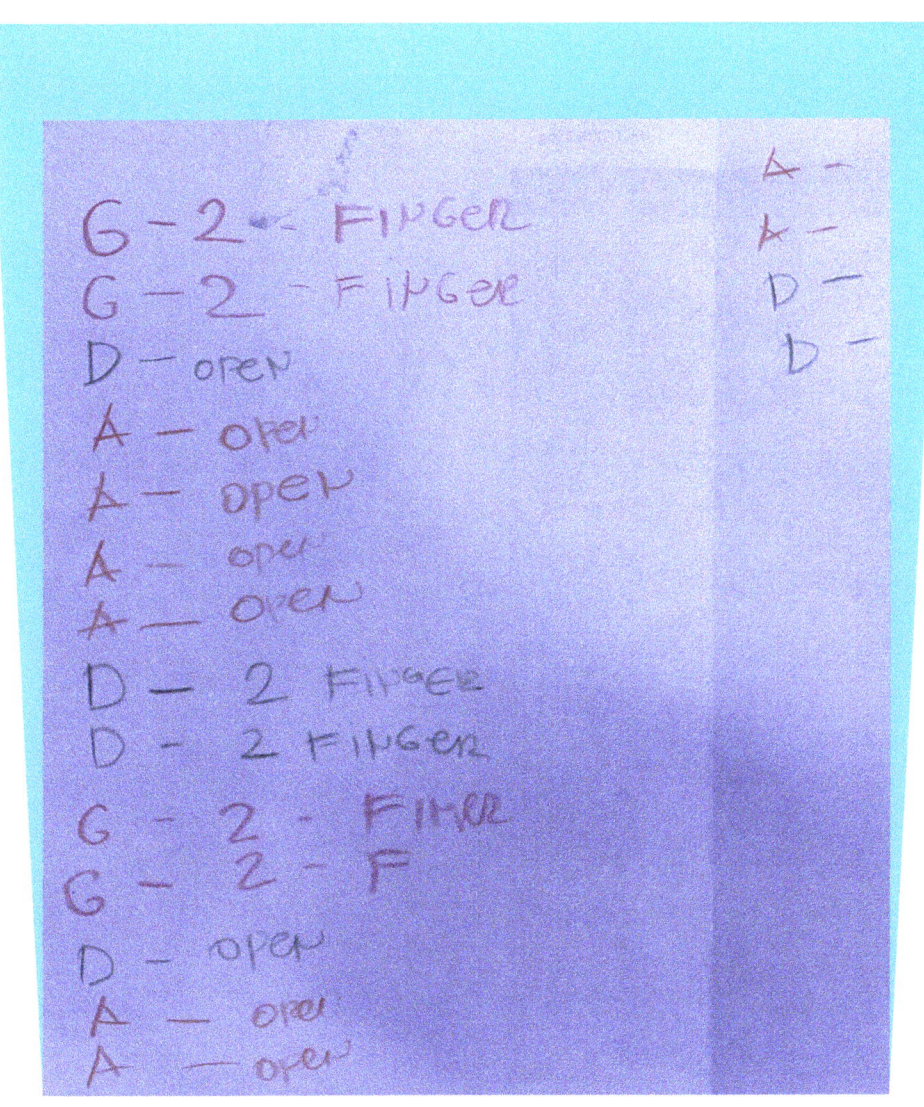

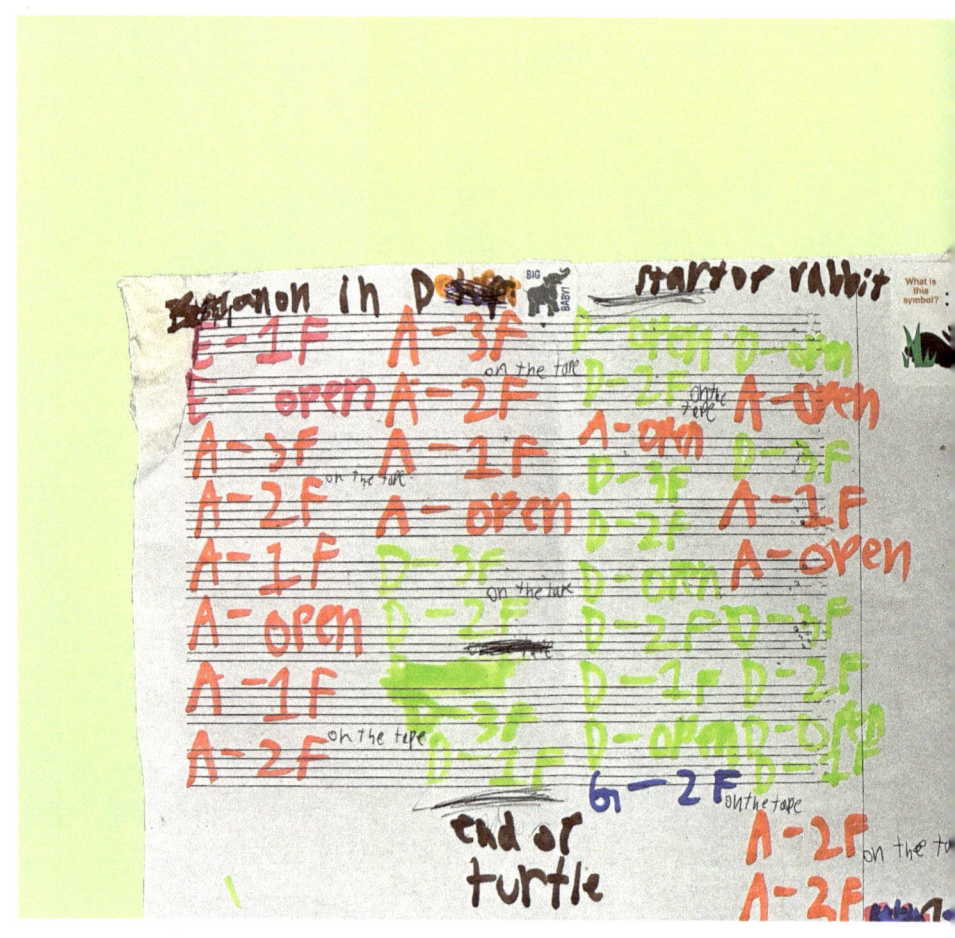

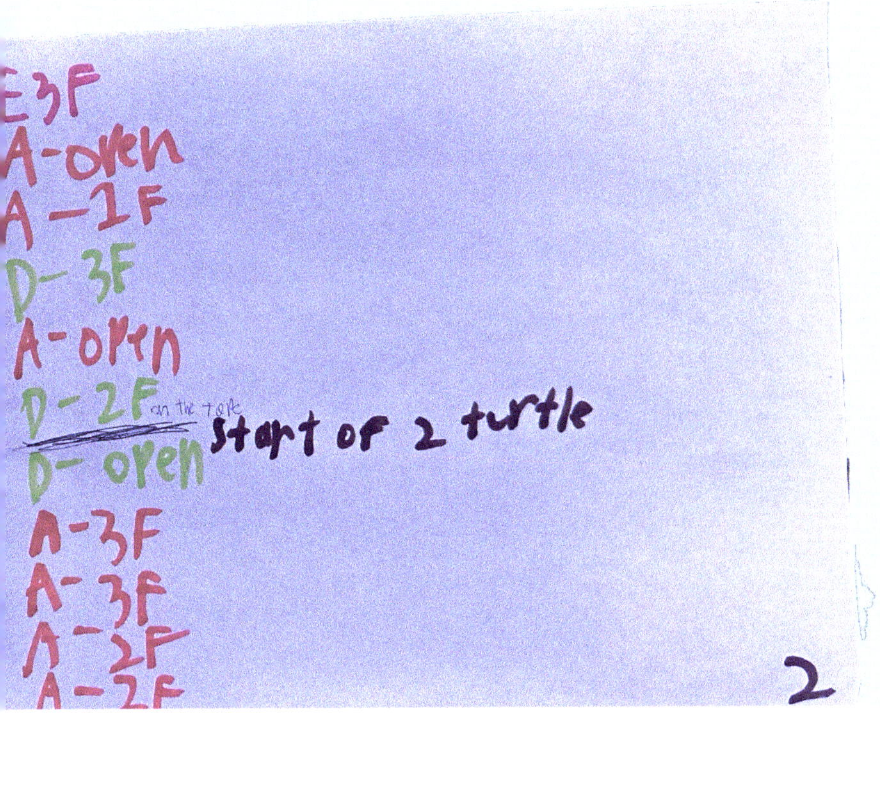

E3F
A-open
A-1F
D-3F
A-open
D-2F on the top ~~start of 2 turtle~~
D-open
A-3F
A-3F
A-2F
A-2F

2

Composing on Paper

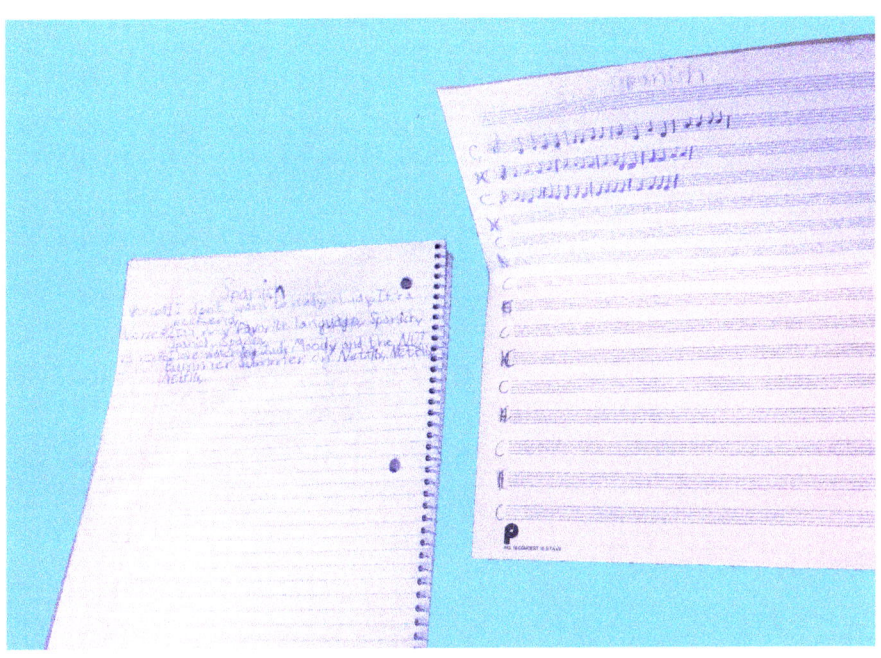

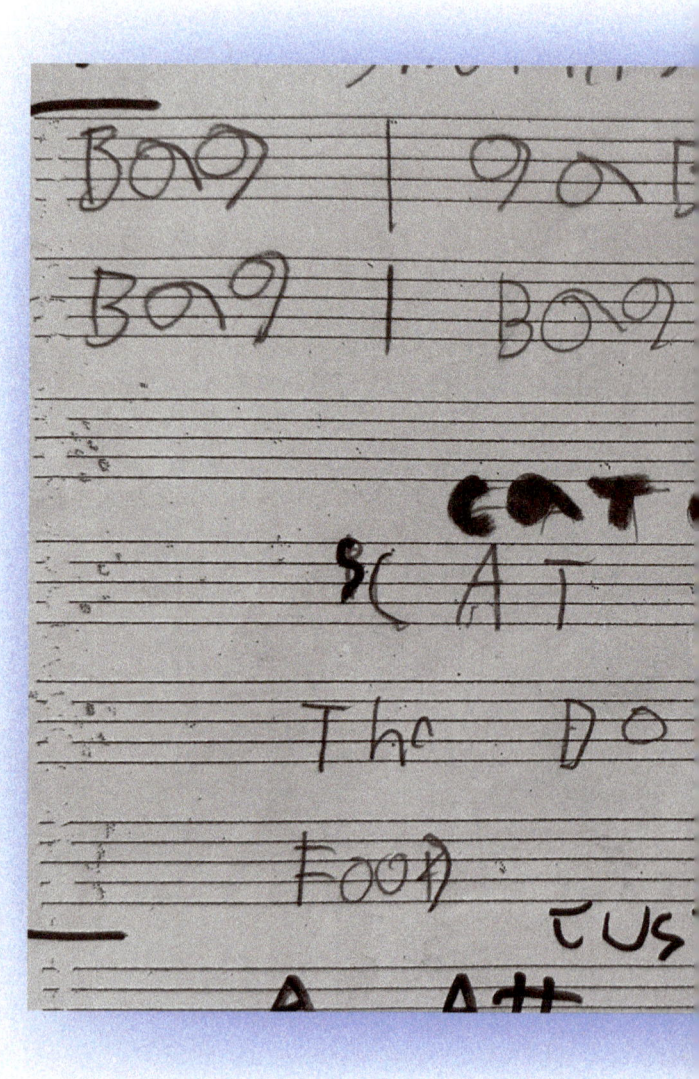

On Music Education, Psychology & Different Abilities

```
    4
1  FFFF
2  FCFE
3  C(low) CCC
4  D CCE

IV

1  ADE
   EDA
   AEDD
   ABA
   CEG
```

My Ipad will
If correctly to school
I would love to
introduce it to you

I think you just
drew out and feel
his rubber case
                    Dorien wore jeans

And try over 4 for 23 hours

Instrumental bridge
(soft fades will turn to +
sing)

Ha Ha Ha   A
This was avery Dorien
Ha Ha Ha
wo, It turns audience

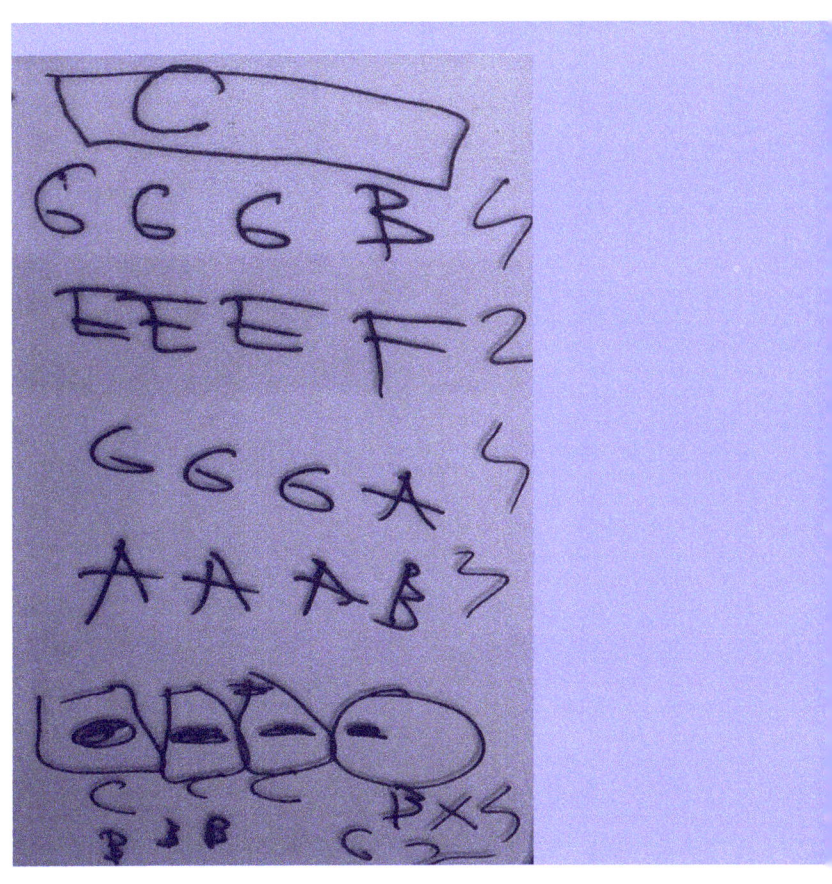

On Music Education, Psychology & Different Abilities

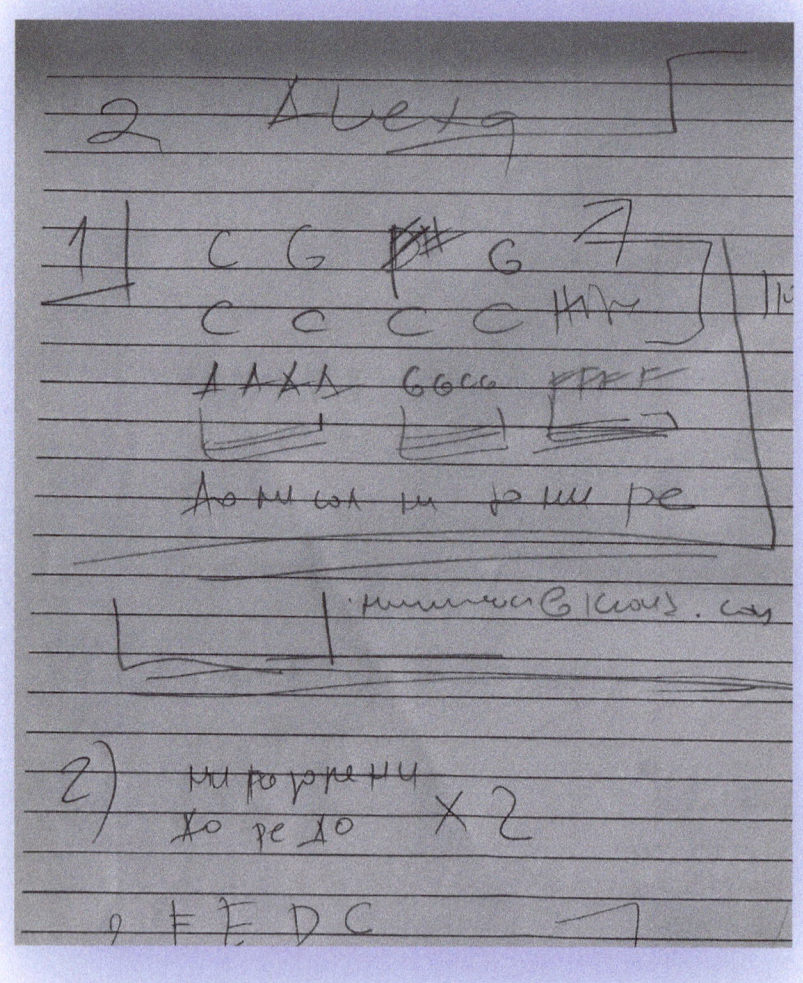

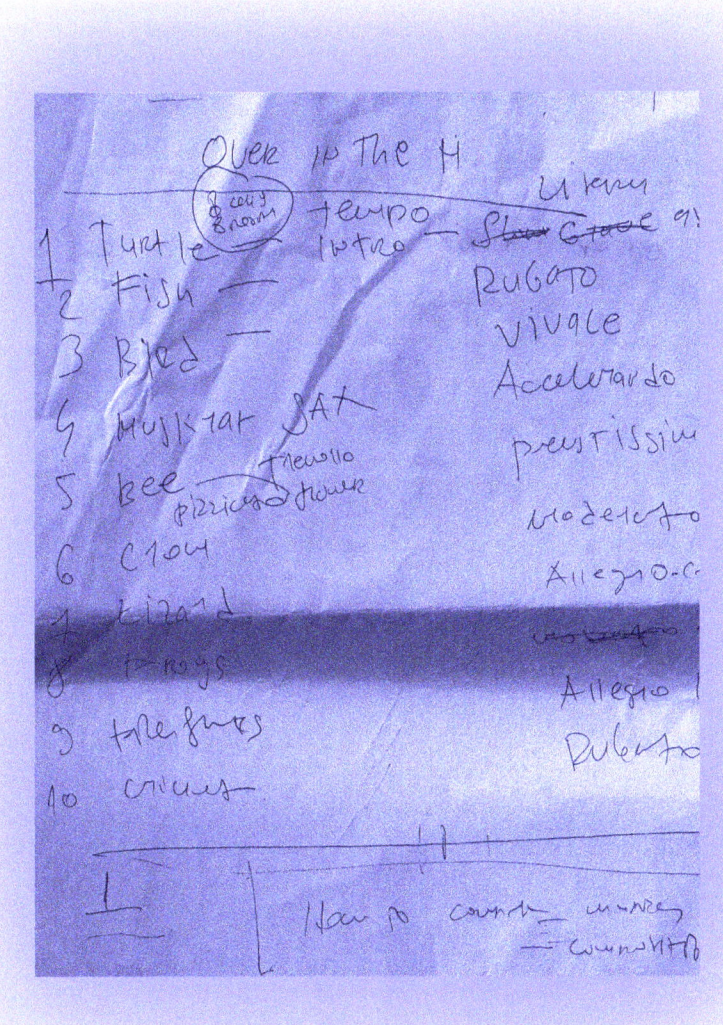

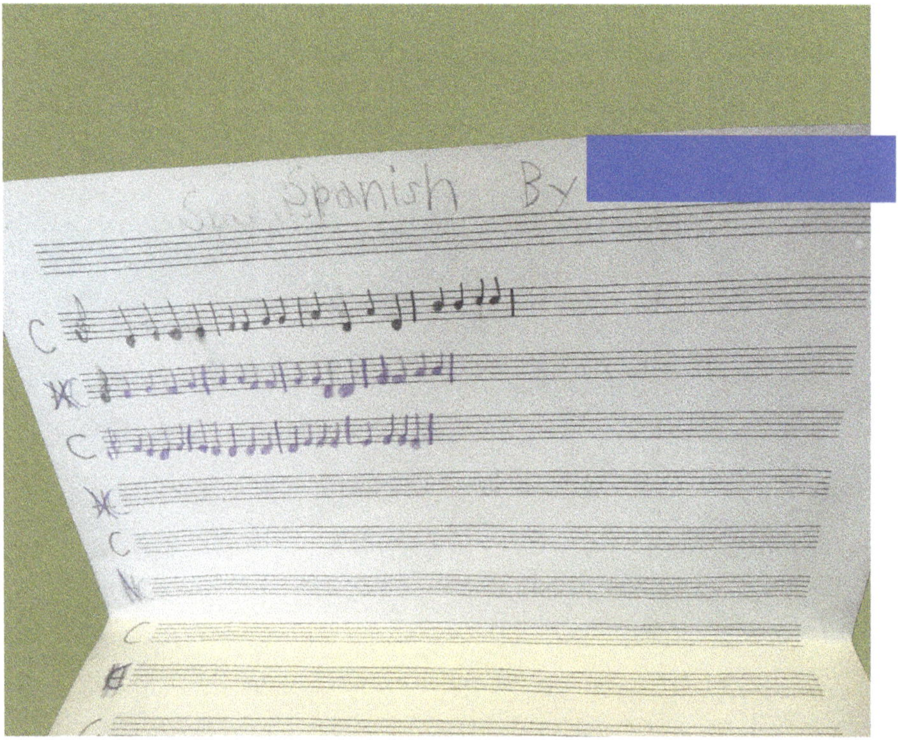

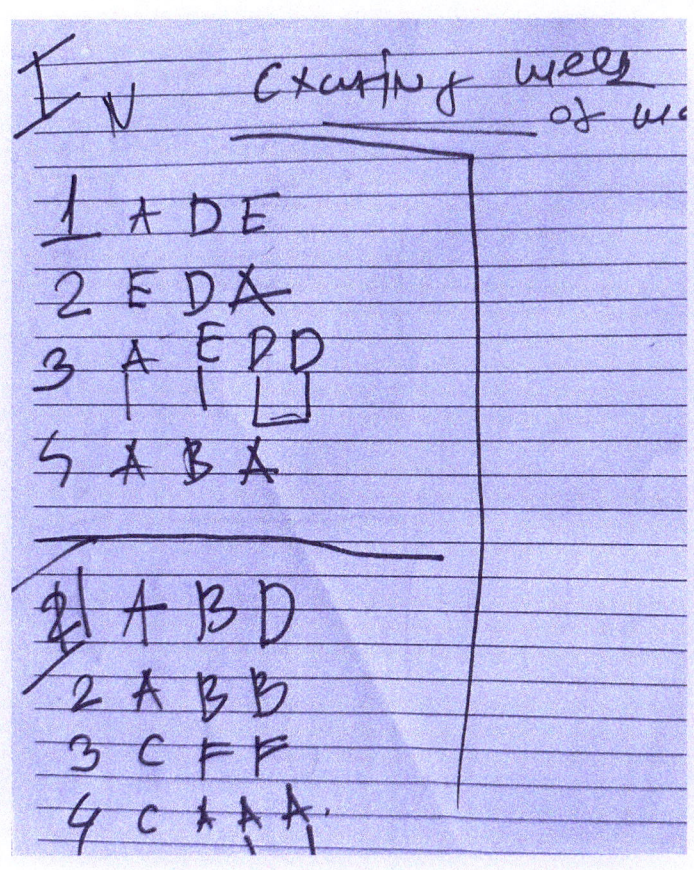

On Music Education, Psychology & Different Abilities

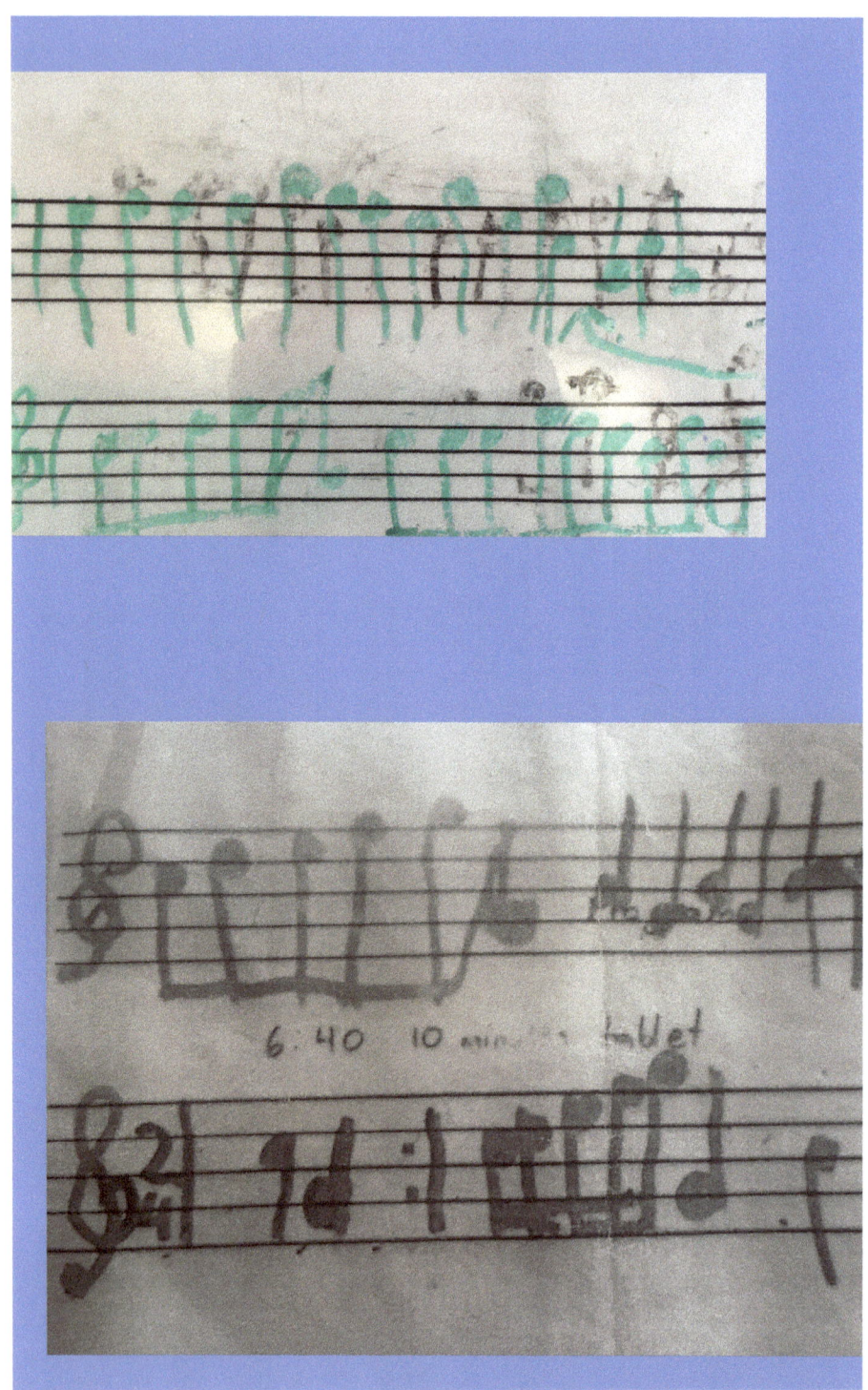

Sofija Zlatanova

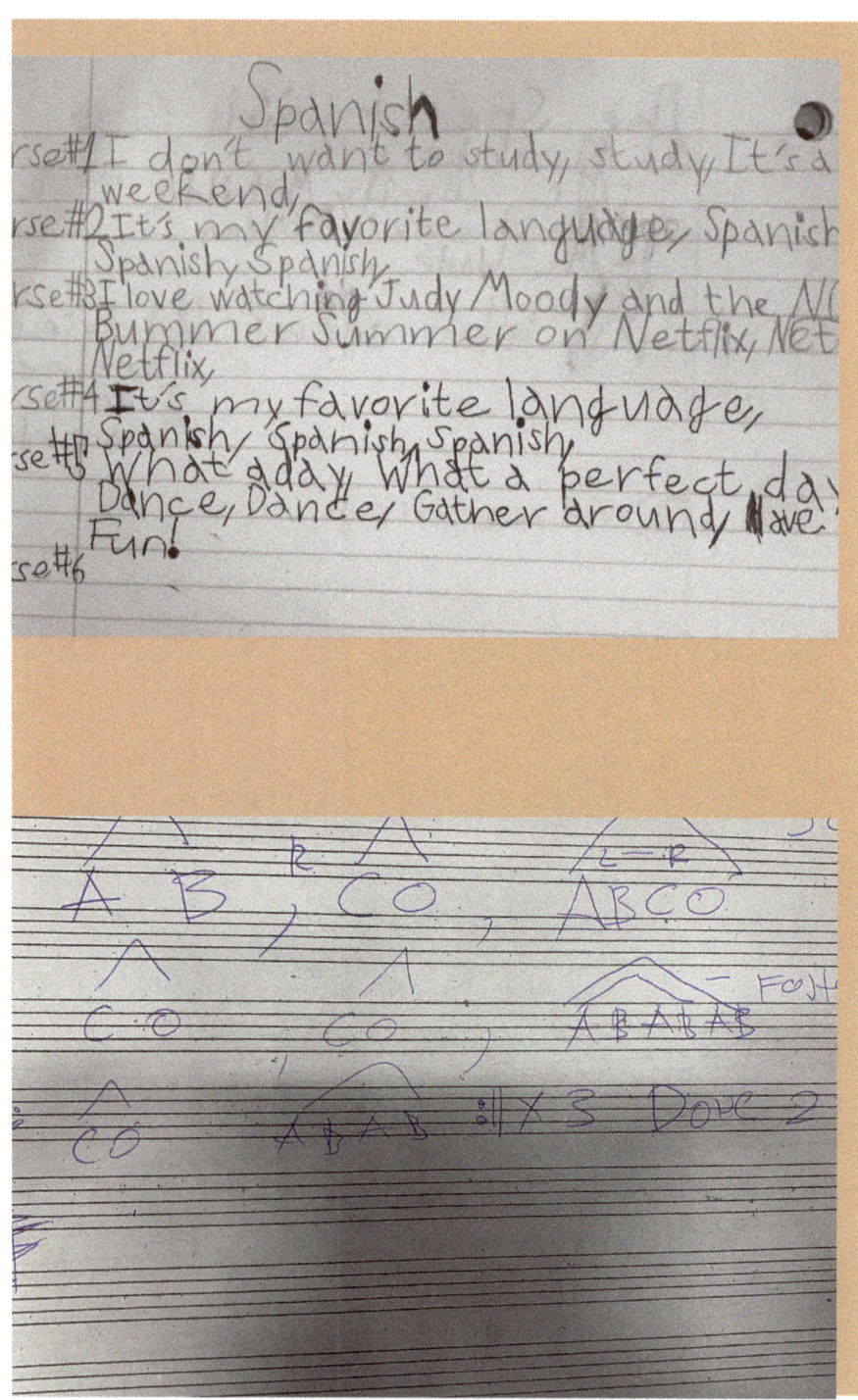

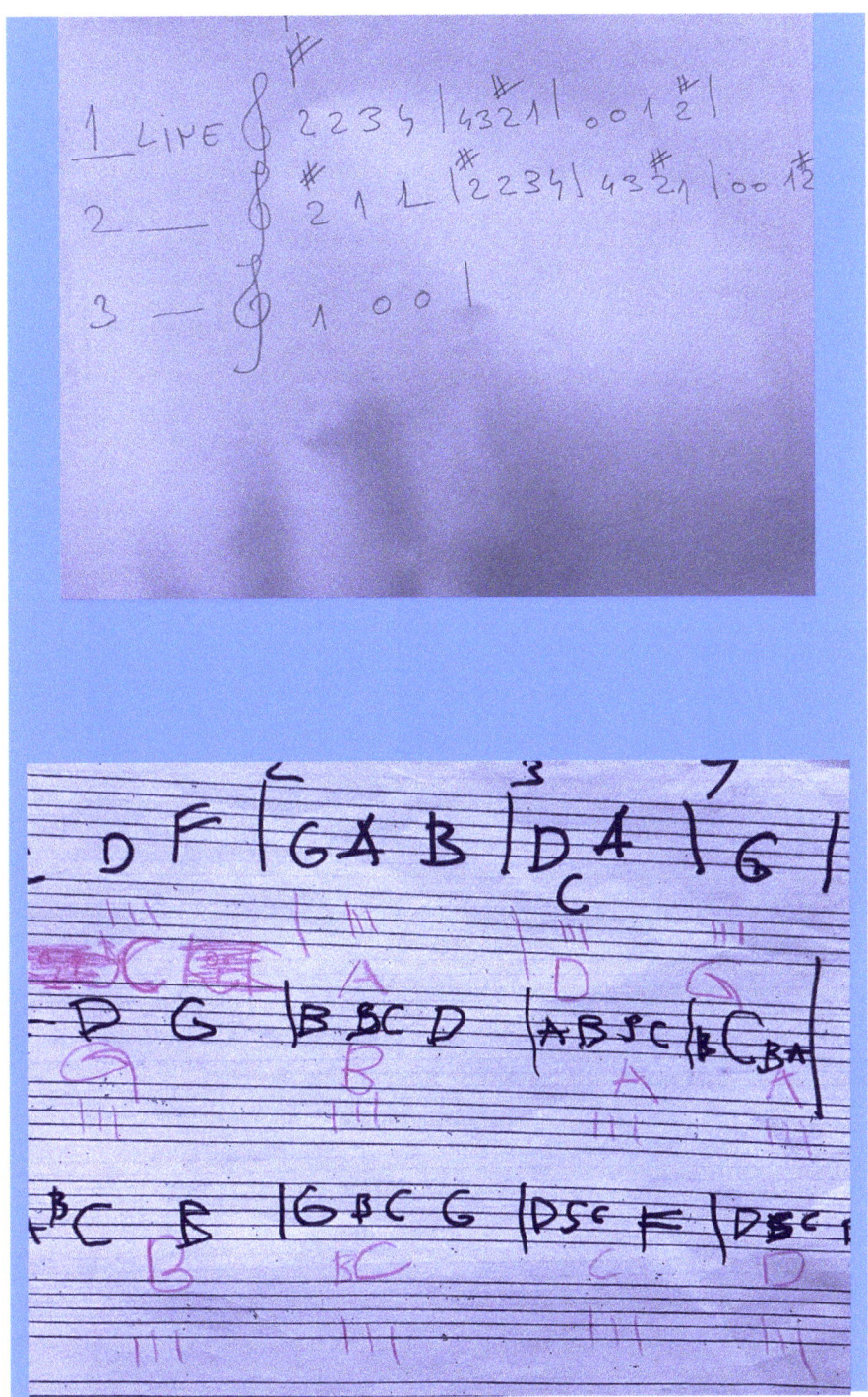

On Music Education, Psychology & Different Abilities

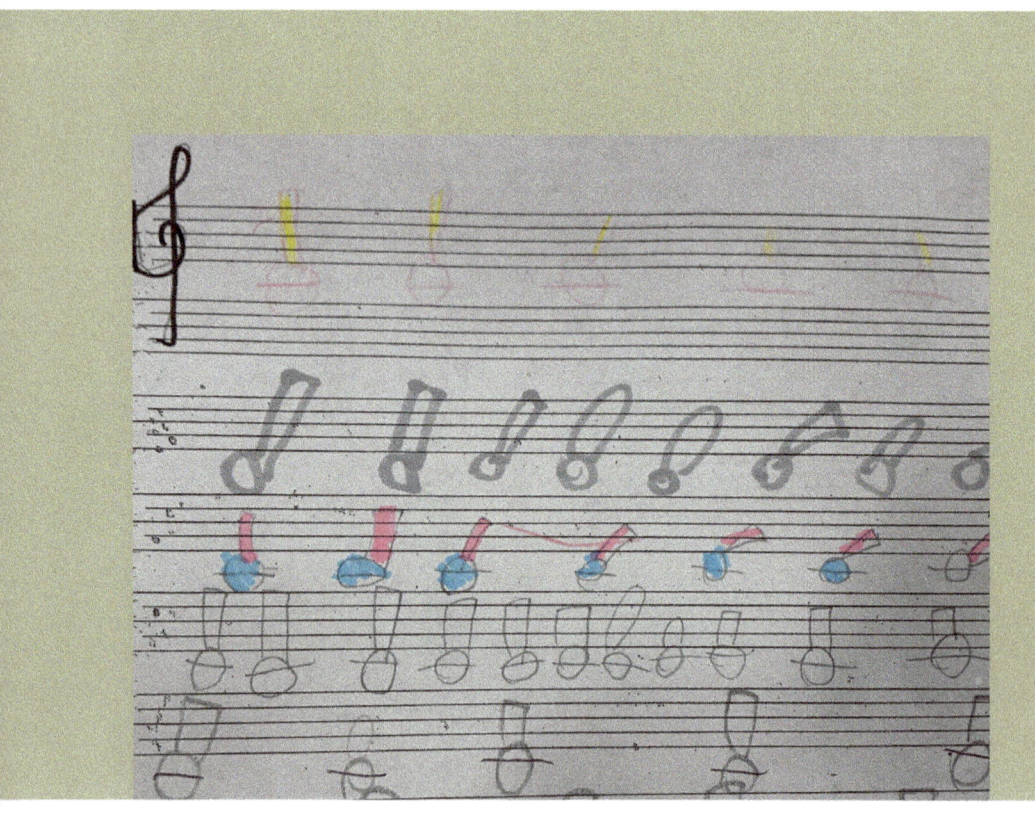

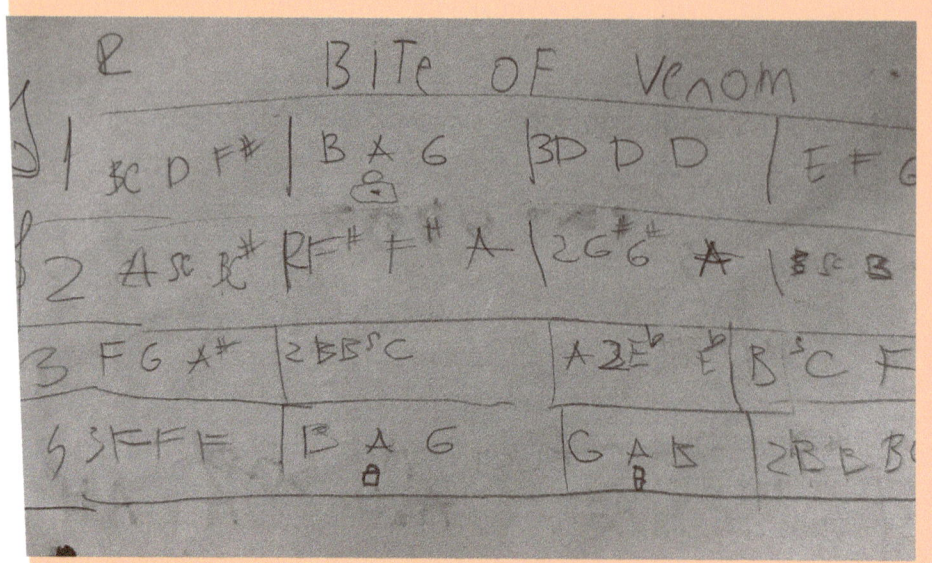

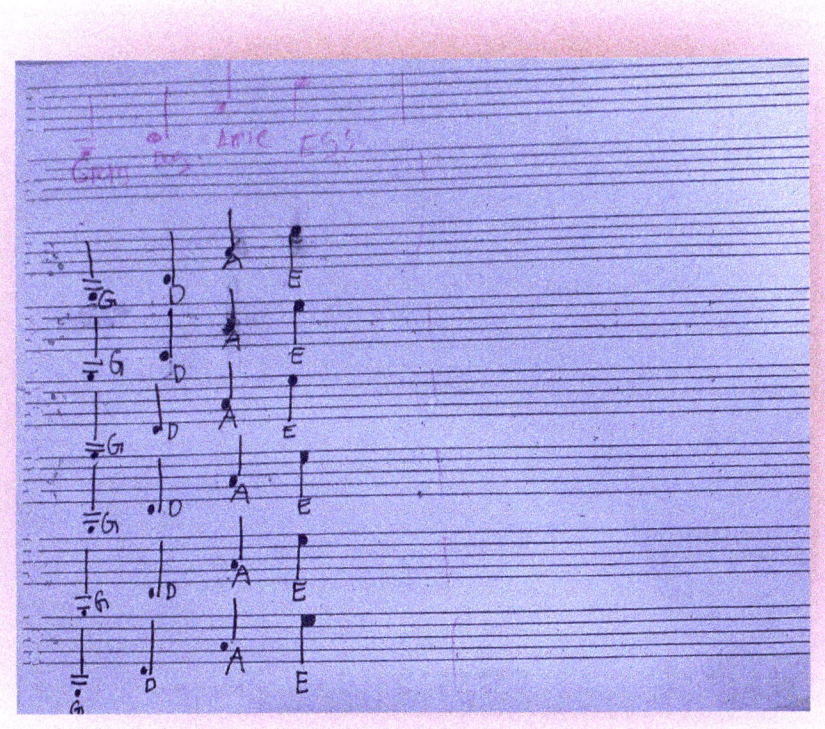

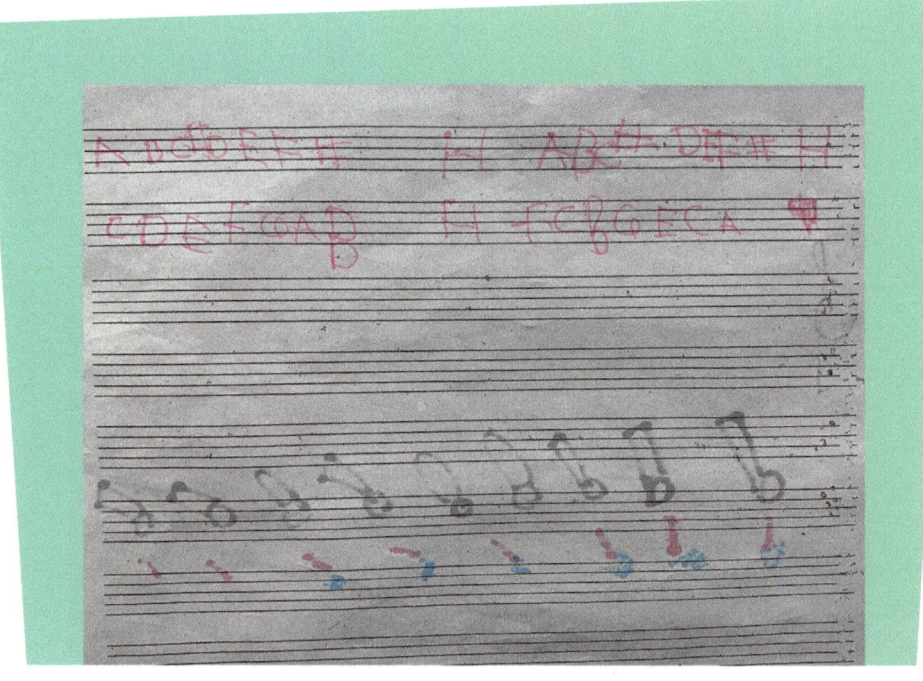

Sofija Zlatanova

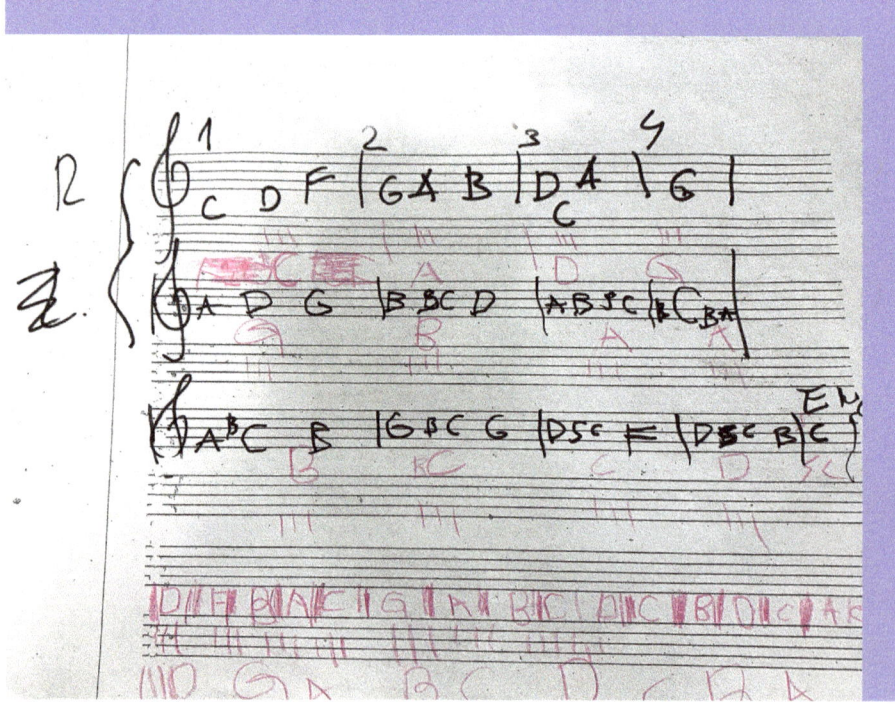

Sofija Zlatanova

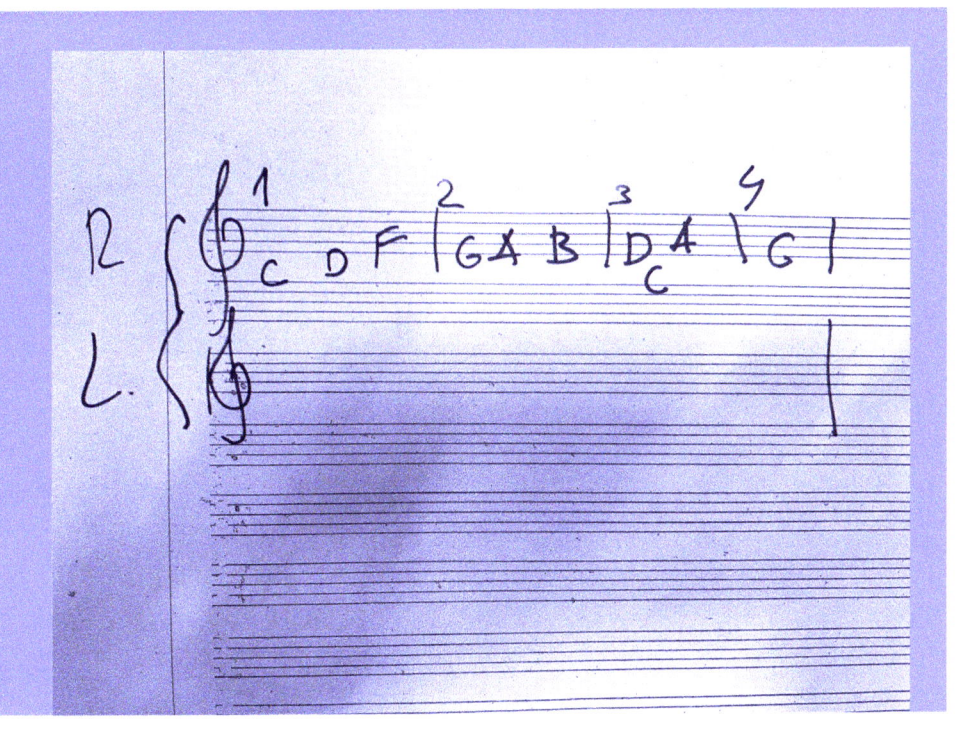

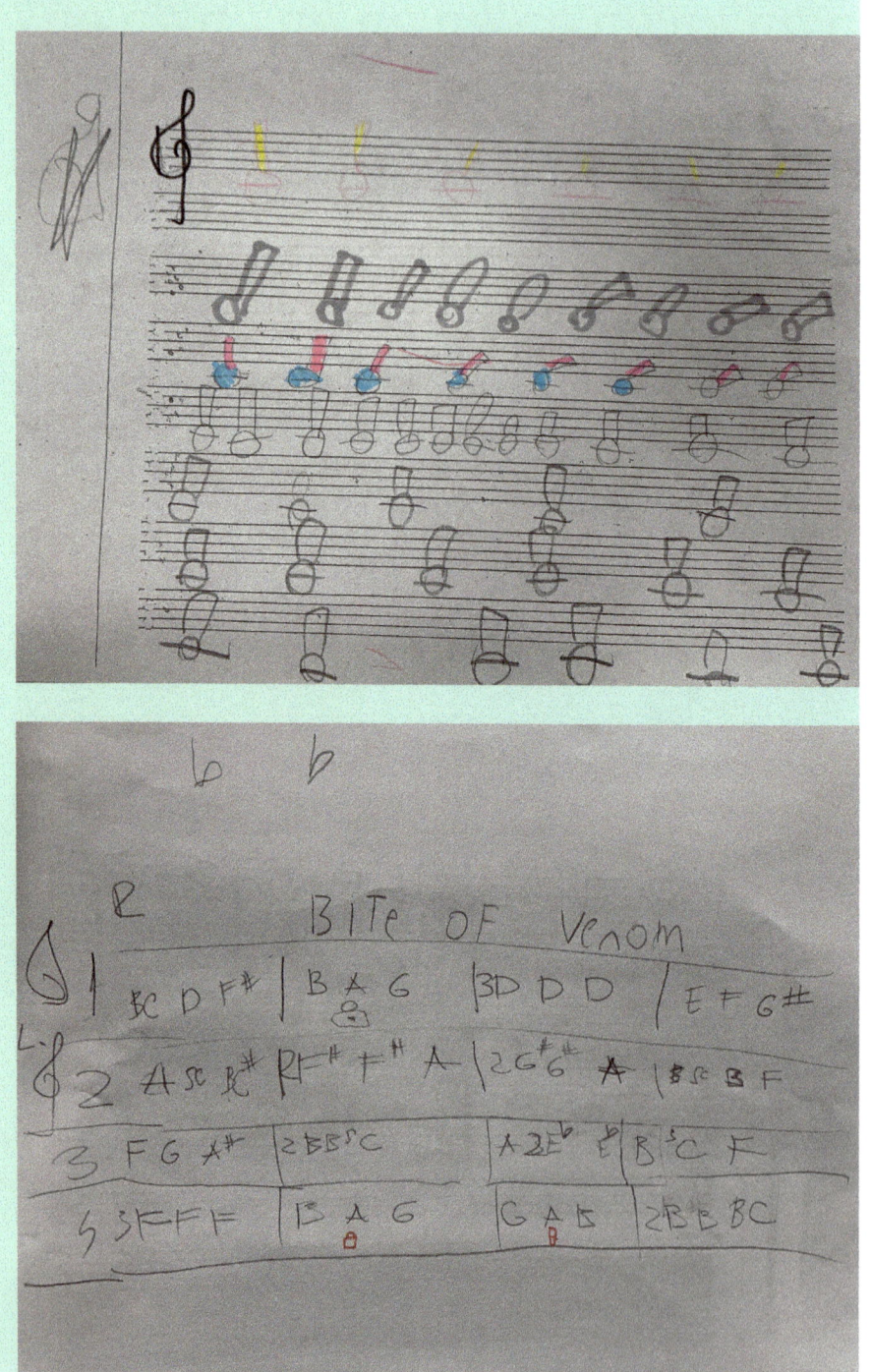

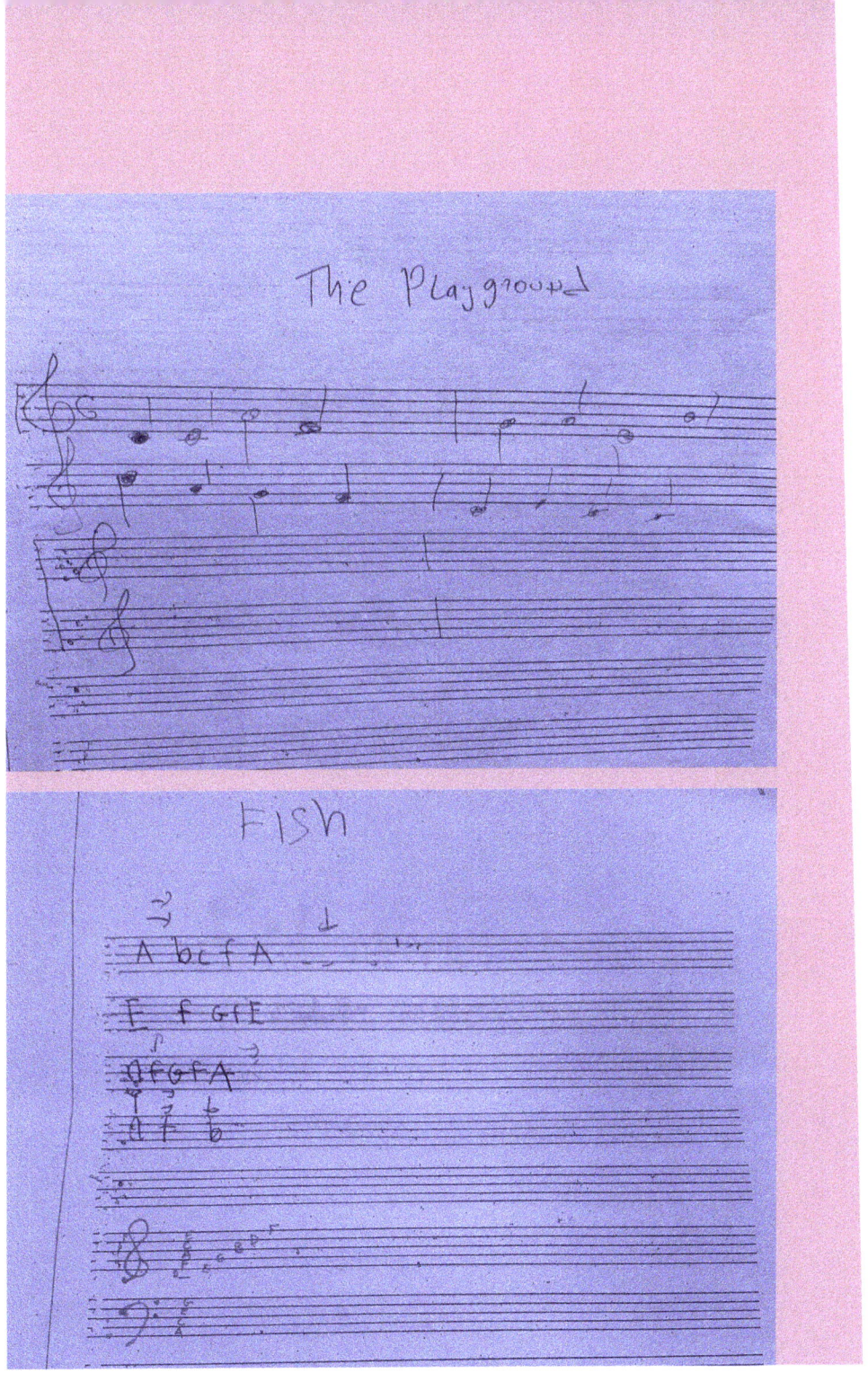

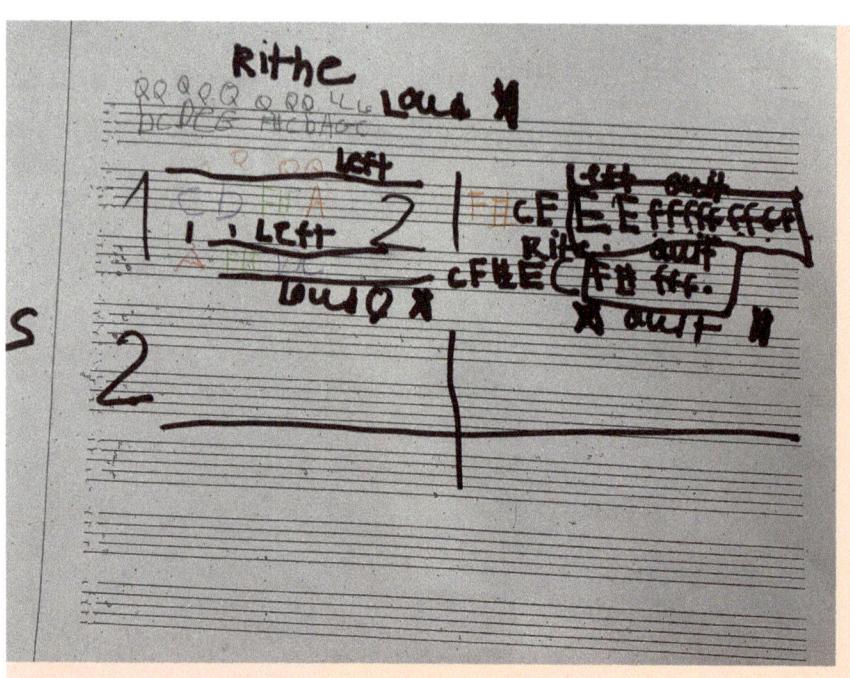

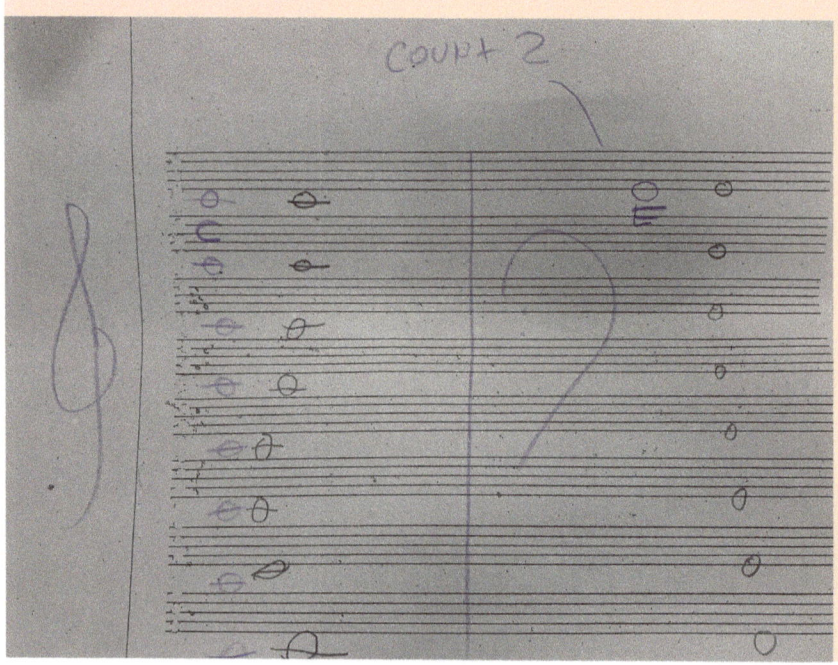

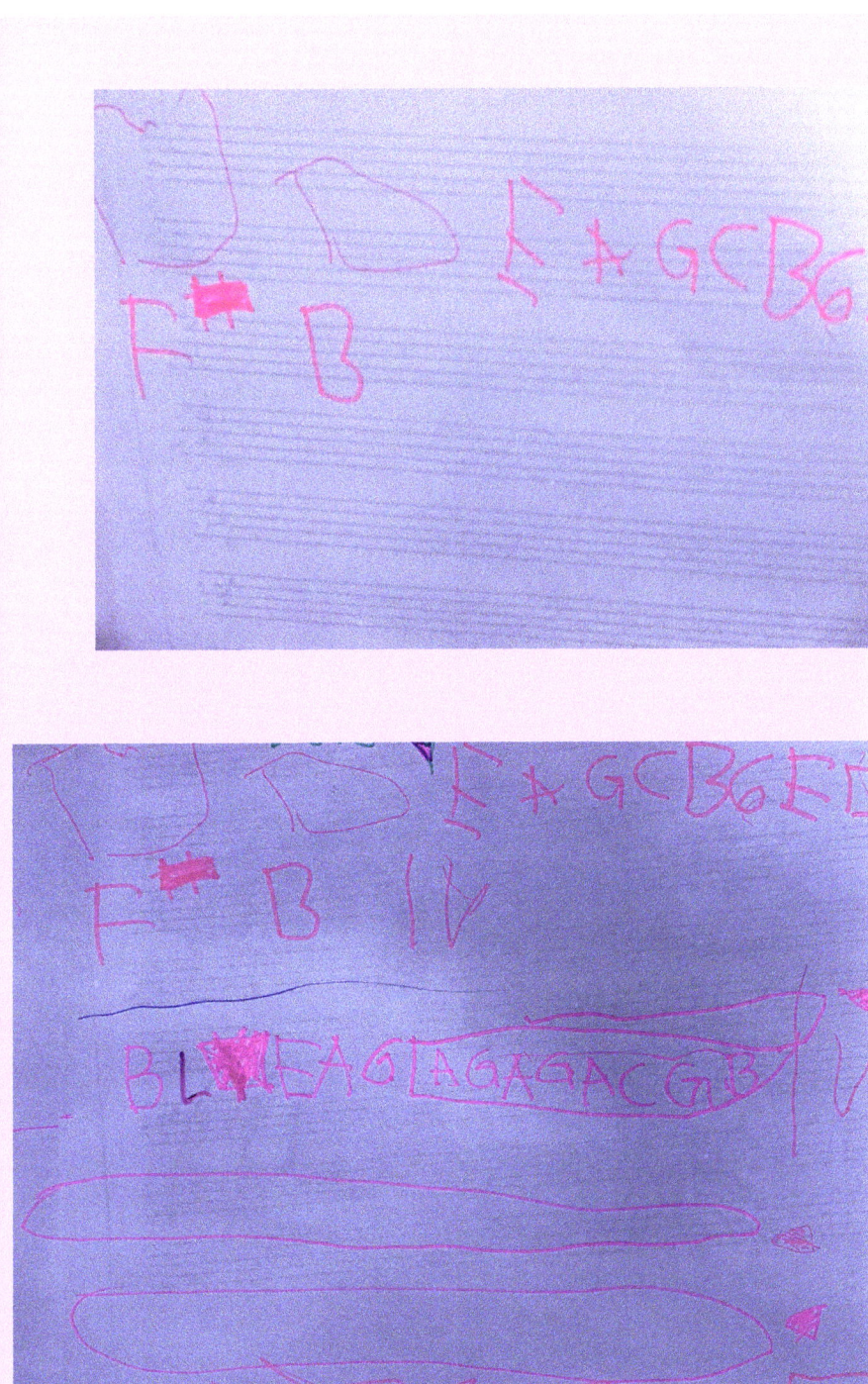

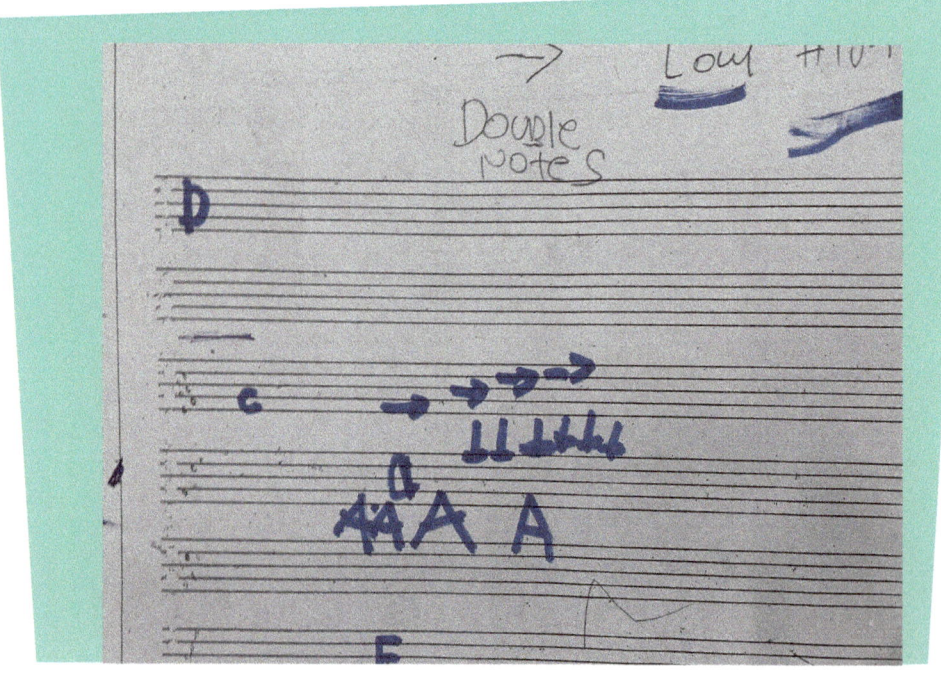

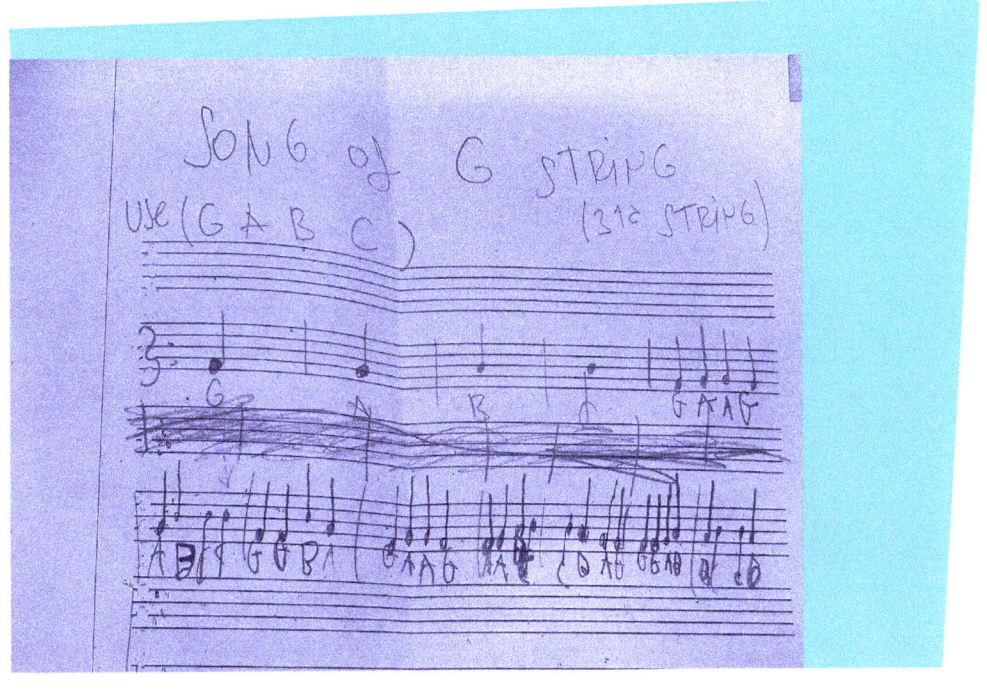

Acknowledgments

The moment we stop worrying about the opinions of others and conforming to societal norms, we unlock the power to be fearless and immortal. This liberation allows us to grow: and, like a flower, education will thrive when it is nurtured and allowed to improve.

Nature responds to our new-found freedom by enabling us to create and innovate. The seasons of spring, summer, autumn, and winter sustain us as we continue to explore and expand our potential.

I want to express my gratitude to each and every one of you. From the moment of your birth, you possess a unique combination of talents and intelligence. My wish is for you to embrace your distinctiveness and have the courage to explore what makes you special. You are already beautiful and unique just as you are.

Sofija

I also want to thank and acknowledge the following people:

My Students.

My professors from Boston Conservatory at Berklee: Prof. Dr. Rhoda Bernard, and Prof Dr. Alice M. Hammel who inspired me.

Valentina Samac.

My editor, Penny Silva, and Interior and Book Designer, Jackie Briggs.

My daughter, Hiba, and my husband, Mounir.

My mother, Makedonka, my brother, Boshko, and my father, Slobodan—who flew overseas to help me with my daughter so that I could complete this book.

Bibliography

CHAPTER 1

Baillot, Pierre. *The Art of the Violin* **(1991).** Retrieved from https://www.google.com/books/edition/The_Art_of_the_Violin/OlE CgAAQBAJ?hl=en&gbpv=1

Boyden, D. D. (1990). *The History of Violin Playing from its Origins to 1761: and its Relationship to the Violin and Violin Music* **(Clarendon Paperbacks, Later Printing). Oxford: Clarendon Press.**

Brown, H., & Boyden, D. D. (1966). 'The History of Violin Playing from its Origins to 1761 and its Relationship to the Violin and Violin Music'. *Notes,* 23(1). Retrieved from https://doi.org/10.2307/895139

Corelli, Arcangelo. **(pdf)** *How might Arcangelo Corelli have played the violin?* (n.d.). ResearchGate.

Courvoisier, Carl. (1908). *Technics of Violin Playing on Joachim's Method.* **Retrieved from Scribd.** https://www.scribd.com/document/146733782/Technics-of-Violin-Playing

Kolneder, Walter **[PDF]. (2010).** Retrieved from http://dl.booktolearn.com/ebooks2/art/music/9781574670387_the_amadeus_book_of_the_violin_9ed2.pdf

DeLay, Dorothy. (2002) Piet Koornhof, 'Sweet Genius' in *Musicus* **29(2)** *p.* **65. Retrieved from**

http://www.pietkoornhof.com/uploads/8/4/1/5/8415949/sweet_genius_musicus_v29_n2_a11.pdf

DeLay, Dorothy. Wikipedia. (n.d.). https://en.wikipedia.org/wiki/Dorothy_DeLay

DeLay, Dorothy (quote) *"Children become what they are told they are"* **(n.d.).** Retrieved from https://quotefancy.com/quote/1675835/Dorothy-DeLay-Children-become-what-they-are-told-they-are

Eanes, Edward. (2013). *Auer, Leopold (in the United States).* Retrieved from https://www.oxfordmusiconline.com/grovemusic/view/10.1093/gmo/9781561592630.001.0001/omo-9781561592630-e-1002248175

Einstein, Albert. (2016). Classic FM, August 3. Retrieved from https://www.classicfm.com/discover-music/latest/quotes-about-classical-music/albert-einstein/

Einstein, Albert. (2017). *Inside Einstein's love affair with Lina.* **National Geographic. Feb. Retrieved from** https://www.nationalgeographic.com/news/2017/02/einstein-genius-violin-music-physics-science/

Galamian, Ivan. (1999). *Principles of Violin Playing and Teaching* **(3rd edn). Shar Products Co.**

Geminiani, Francesco. (1751). *The Art of Playing on the Violin.* **(Facsimile edn, 1951.) Oxford: Oxford University Press.**

Heifetz, Jascha. **Wikipedia. (n.d.).** https://en.wikipedia.org/wiki/Jascha_Heifetz

Heifetz, Jascha. (quotes: n.d.). BrainyQuote. Retrieved from https://www.brainyquote.com/quotes/jascha_heifetz_114403

Joachim, Joseph. **Wikipedia. (n.d.).** https://en.wikipedia.org/wiki/Joseph_Joachim

Kreutzer, Rodolphe. **Wikipedia. (n.d.).** https://en.wikipedia.org/wiki/Rodolphe_Kreutzer

Mozart, Leopold, & **Editha Knocker (ed.).** *A Treatise on the Fundamental Principles of Violin Playing.* **(1949).**

Mozart, Leopold, & Editha Knocker (ed.) (1986). 'A treatise on the fundamental principles of violin playing'. *Journal of the American Musicological Society*, *2***(3).**

Mozart, Leopold. *A Treatise on the Fundamental Principles of Violin Playing.* **(1985).** Retrieved from https://www.google.com/books/edition/A_Treatise_on_the_Fundamental_Principles/kRweNZB-37KUC?hl=en&gbpv=1

Mozart, Leopold. (quotes: n.d.). Retrieved from http://www.notable-quotes.com/m/mozart_quotes.html

Perepelitsa, M. (2016, 6 September). *Classical music's pedagogue: Stolyarsk.* **Odessa Review, 6 September. Retrieved from** http://odessareview.com/classical-musics-pedagogue-stolyarsky/

Pollow, Andrew. (2011) *Old Russian School Left Hand.* **Violinist.com, 8 June. Retrieved from https://www.violinist.com/discussion/archive/20318/**

Schueneman, B. R., & W. E. Studwell (ed.) (2002). *The French Violin School: Viotti, Rode,*

Kreutzer, Baillot and their Contemporaries. **The Lyre Of Orpheus Press.**

Stephane Grappelli **(quote.) (n.d.). Retrieved from** https://www.apassion-4jazz.net/quotations5.html

Veracini, Francesco Maria (1744). **ResearchGate. (2014, 1 January).** Retrieved from https://www.researchgate.net/figure/Francesco-Maria-Veracini-op-2-1744_fig3_296694493

CHAPTER 2

Clive, H. P. (2001). *Beethoven and his world: a biographical dictionary.* **New York: Oxford University Press. Retrieved from** http://books.google.mk/books?id=v0597Beh43EC&printsec=frontcover#v=onepage&q&f=false

Lebrecht, N. (1985). *Book of musical anecdotes.* **New York: Simon & Schuster. Retrieved from**

http://books.google.mk/books?id=YlT5qecRIMsC&printsec=frontcover#v=onepage&q&f=false

Munteanu, I. (2004-2014). *All about Beethoven.* **Retrieved from** http://www.all-about-beethoven.com/beethovenmusic.html

Munteanu, I. (2004-2014). *Heiligenstadt Testament (October 6, 1802) to his brothers.* **Retrieved from**

http://www.all-about-beethoven.com/heiligenstadt_test.html

Sullivan, J. W. N. (1936). *Beethoven—His spiritual development.* **New York: Alfred A. Knopf. Retrieved from**

https://archive.org/details/beethovenhisspir002615mbp

Thayer A. W. *The life of Ludwig van Beethoven*, **Vol. 2. New York: The Beethoven Association. Retrieved from** www.gutenberg.org/ebooks/43592

Environmental and Nature

https://pubs.acs.org/journal/esthag https://www.live-science.com/36735-does-the-color-green-boost-exercise-s-effects.html

https://www.livescience.com/32496-why-is-grass-green.html

Physical Activity

https://www.insider.com/health-benefits-of-running-2018-9

https://www.mayoclinic.org/diseases-conditions/depression/in-depth/depression-and-exercise/art-20046495

Nutrition

https://www.mayoclinic.org/healthy-lifestyle/nutrition-and-healthy-eating/in-depth/caffeine/art-20049372

https://www.ncbi.nlm.nih.gov/pmc/articles/PMC6617169/

http://web.colby.edu/st297-global18/2018/10/28/serotonin-dopamine-the-neurological-benefits-of-chocolate/

https://exploringyourmind.com/7-foods-serotonin-dopamine/

CHAPTER 3

https://www.researchgate.net/publication/265261482 (A Style of Music Characterized by Fibonacci and the Golden Ratio, by Casey Mongoven)

https://hrcak.srce.hr/file/223111 (Anxieties and Depression Disorders in Composers) *(1)* Croatian Physicians´ Music Society, C.M.A., Zagreb, Croatia; *(2)* University Department of Psychiatry, Sestre Milosrdnice University Hospital Center, Zagreb, Croatia.

Interview: Nikola Tesla and John Smith (from the American magazine *Immortality*).

https://www.mayoclinic.org/healthy-lifestyle/nutrition-and-healthy-eating/in-depth/caffeine/art-20049372

https://www.naxos.com/sharedfiles/PDF/8.553311_sungtext.pdf

https://hekint.org/2021/11/30/bela-bartok-1881-1945-the-years-in-america-triumph-over-tragedy/

McDowell, C. (2010). An adaptation toolkit for teaching music. TEACHING Exceptional Children Plus, 6(3). Retrieved from

http://escholarship.bc.edu/education/tecplus/vol6/iss3/art3

CHAPTER 4

Hendry, E. R. (2010, April 30). Scanning a Stradivarius. Smithsonian Magazine. Retrieved from https://www.smithsonianmag.com/smithsonian-institution/scanning-a-stradivarius 13807009/

https://journals.sagepub.com/doi/full/10.1177/2059204318769639

http://www.artsedsearch.org/summaries/short-term-music-training-enhances-verbal- intelligence-and-executive-function

http://www.nydailynews.com/life-style/health/film-music-power-alzheimer-patients-article- 1.1580719

http://www.sciencedaily.com/releases/2009/02/090223221230.htm

http://www.huffingtonpost.com/rita-altman-rn/music-and-memory_b_3639805.html

http://www.psmag.com/news/do-re-mi-promotes-a-feeling-of-we-19058/

http://www.psychology.mcmaster.ca/ljt/GerryUnrauTrainor_2012.pdf

http://www.soc.northwestern.edu/brainvolts/documents/Tierney_Kraus_Chapter_2014.pdf

http://www.psychology.mcmaster.ca/ljt/anvari_et_al_2002.pdf

Image gallery

Some of the literature used in Assisted Various Tools for Different Learning Styles:

Fretless Finger Guides

Over in the Meadow by Olive A. Wadsworth

Music for Little Mozarts Workbook 1 by C.H. Barden, G. Kowalchyk, E.L. Lancaster

Note Designs by J.S. Bastien

PreTime Piano Classics arranged by Faber & Faber

BLUE BOOK of TUNES: Violin: A First Book for Violin by Bonnie Greene

Great Composers Coloring Book (Dover History Coloring Book)